Second Edition

Starting Strong

This book is dedicated to those teachers and colleagues who touched my life, both as a student and as a teacher. To name a few, Miss Nordyke (fourth grade), Steve White (sixth grade), Mr. and Mrs. Bugh (middle school), and Mrs. Mahoney, Jeff and Bobbi Kramer, and Chuck Grande (high school). There are more that should be mentioned, yet these teachers inspired me to learn, challenge myself, and laugh. I also dedicate this book to the many teacher colleagues I have been blessed to share staff lounges and short lunches with. Marilynn Montgomery, Lee Watson, and Susan Blakely have been and are at the top of this list for sharing their passion and skills as an educator with me and helping to keep my teaching fire lit. Last but certainly not least, I dedicate this book to my parents, June and Gordon Nicholson. Both retired high school teachers, they instilled in me not only the importance of learning but the pure joy of it. They have been and continue to be my two best and favorite teachers of all.

—Kristen J. Nelson

I am one of those people who fell into teaching by accident. What turned this accident into a lifelong passion, however, are two things: first, my students, who taught me more than I could possibly teach them, and second, the many gifted and dedicated educators who willingly shared their talents, enthusiasm, and knowledge on behalf of student learning. I dedicate this book to them and my circle of friends and family, who have provided me with continuous support throughout my career and honored my "accidental" profession with their respect and encouragement.

—Kim Bailey

Second Edition

Starting Strong

Surviving and Thriving as a New Teacher

Kristen J. Nelson • Kim Bailey

CORWIN PRESS
A SAGE Publications Company
Thousand Oaks, CA 91320

Copyright © 2008 by Corwin Press.

For information:

Corwin Press
A Sage Publications Company
2455 Teller Road
Thousand Oaks, California 91320
www.corwinpress.com

Sage Publications Ltd.
1 Oliver's Yard
55 City Road
London EC1Y 1SP
United Kingdom

Sage Publications India Pvt. Ltd.
B 1/I 1 Mohan Cooperative
    Industrial Area
Mathura Road, New Delhi 110 044
India

Sage Publications Asia-Pacific Pte. Ltd.
33 Pekin Street #02-01
Far East Square
Singapore 048763

Printed in the United States of America

Library of Congress Cataloging-in-Publication Data

Nelson, Kristen.
Starting strong: Surviving and thriving as a new teacher/Kristen J. Nelson, Kim Bailey.—2nd ed.
    p. cm.
Includes bibliographical references and index.
ISBN 978-1-4129-5561-4 (cloth)
ISBN 978-1-4129-5562-1 (pbk.)
    1. First year teachers—United States. 2. Teacher effectiveness—United States.
3. Effective teaching—United States. I. Bailey, Kim. II. Title.

LB2844.1.N4N45 2008
371.1—dc22   2007008781

This book is printed on acid-free paper.

07   08   09   10   11   10 9   8   7   6   5   4   3   2   1

Acquisitions Editor:	Hudson Perigo
Editorial Assistant:	Jordan Barbakow
Production Editor:	Melanie Birdsall
Typesetter:	C&M Digitals (P) Ltd.
Copy Editor:	Bonnie Freeman
Proofreader:	Andrea Martin
Indexer:	Marilyn Augst
Cover Designer:	Scott Van Atta

Contents

Acknowledgments

Corwin Press gratefully acknowledges the contributions of the following reviewers:

Donna R. Bohannon
Teacher Induction Staff Development Coordinator
Memphis City Schools
Memphis, TN

Lori Grossman
Instructional Coordinator
Professional Development Services
Houston Independent School District
Houston, TX

Greg Keith
Teacher Induction Staff Development Coordinator
Memphis City Schools
Memphis, TN

Elaine Mayer
Lead New Teacher Coach
Oakland Unified School District
Oakland, CA

Laurie VanSteenkiste
Staff Development Consultant
Macomb Intermediate School District
Clinton Township, MI

About the Authors

Kristen J. Nelson is the author of numerous books in the education field, including *Teaching in the Digital Age* and *Developing Students' Multiple Intelligences*. She works for a large suburban school district in Orange County, California. Mrs. Nelson was an elementary and middle school teacher before becoming an educational administrator. She lives with her husband and two daughters in San Clemente, California.

Kim Bailey, with more than 29 years' experience in education, has served as a special education classroom teacher, district administrator, educational consultant, and university professor. For the past eight years, she has placed her professional focus in the areas of professional development and educational leadership. She lives with her husband and family in Southern California.

Introduction

Welcome to teaching. You have entered into one of the most exciting careers you could have chosen and will soon find yourself on an exciting ride. You will have days of exhilaration, days of exhaustion, and days of exhilarating exhaustion. You will have days when your students make you laugh so hard your side hurts and days when your students bring you to tears as you drive home.

You have chosen a career in which no operational manual fits for all teachers. You must find your own way in this career; you must pursue your own unique, individual path.

This book is a survival guide for your first few years of teaching. It features time-tested ideas that will make your first years flow more smoothly. It offers suggestions and advice that will move you quickly past survival mode and help you flourish in this wonderful career called teaching. As you embark on this career, you become a student of the teaching profession. If you put your entire mind, body, and soul into it, you can move out of survival mode quickly and move on into the deeper and richer tasks of daily influencing your students' lives.

Teaching is more than a profession. It is a lifestyle. It calls the brave and strong at heart to enter into a dynamic world of preparing students for a future that is undiscernible.

Teaching has always been a complicated and challenging profession. To many, however, teaching in the early part of the twenty-first century seems far more challenging than was teaching in earlier periods. Information doubles every few months, and the Internet continues to transform the world into a smaller and smaller place. Teachers are asked to embrace this new world for themselves first and then to pass necessary skills on to their students—to teach them to be cognitively flexible and ready for an incomprehensible world. This new millennium calls for a new type of teacher—a teacher who comes to the classroom each day with one eye on the students and the other on the future. Today's teachers recognize that their own intellectual growth is a key component in teaching. They are also willing to sit at the feet of those who have gone before and learn the history before jumping too far into the future.

The Secretary's Commission on Achieving Necessary Skills (SCANS; 1991) was charged by the U.S. Department of Labor with predicting the skills students would need to succeed in the new millennium. SCANS identified five areas of skill competency:

1. Effectively using resources

2. Acquiring and applying information

3. Working with others

4. Working with a variety of technologies

5. Understanding complex interrelationships

SCANS recommended that teachers use a three-fold approach to foster these competencies:

1. Teach basic skills in reading, writing, arithmetic, listening, and speaking

2. Cultivate thinking skills

3. Enhance students' personal qualities (responsibility, self-esteem, sociability, self-management, and integrity)

This is a large bill for any teacher, experienced or new, to fill on a daily basis.

As if preparing students with these skills were not enough, teachers are also called on to build a sense of community for students, to collaborate with colleagues, to supervise technology, to prepare students for high-stakes exams, to help all students meet high standards, to be counselors, and to manage fleeting material resources. Having the skills, knowledge, and motivation to put all these different pieces together in the teaching puzzle does indeed take a special kind of person.

Teaching is not a goal as much as it is a calling. Becoming vice president of the Saturn Car Company is a goal; teaching a young wild thing named Saturn is a calling. This calling is answered in the details, the routines, and the many conversations and discussions that make up a teacher's day. You could have chosen any career you desired, but something in your soul called you to teach—called you to walk into the classroom on a daily basis to nurture and teach souls. It wasn't luck.

It wasn't a wild night in a college pub where everyone shot darts at a career dartboard. It was the fateful calling of a career to you when you drove past the local school with students getting out, running and screaming. It called to you when you saw national statistics on science and math achievement. It called to you when you saw tiny children on a field trip cross the street in front of you, holding hands and being led by a mother hen. It called. You listened. You answered.

Now your job is to be open to what you will learn through this work and to be open to the mysteries of it all. Your job is to find your meaning and identity within the walls of your classroom and the boundaries of your schoolyard. The challenge is to not lose your soul in the busyness and challenges of this calling. There are very few professions that ask for so much—physically, mentally, emotionally, and spiritually. Yet somewhere in the middle of the mayhem, your soul is calling—calling you into the art of teaching and beckoning you to bring your many unique gifts and talents.

Only those who have chosen this profession can understand this calling. Teaching is more than a paycheck, more than a job, and more than something to do during the day. It is soul work—beautiful and satisfying soul work.

HOW THIS BOOK IS ORGANIZED ■

Because you are unique, there is no one way to be a successful teacher, and this book offers no silver bullet. However, this book does provide time-tested ideas and suggestions to help you avoid spending time reinventing the wheel and instead to spend time teaching your children about the origins of the wheel. Multiple roles come with the job title "teacher," and each chapter describes one of these roles.

• Chapter 1, Teacher as a Creator of Classroom Environment, describes *the teacher's role in fostering learning and social growth.* This chapter describes different types of classroom layouts as well as ideas for decorating and arranging the classroom for optimal learning and collaboration.

• Chapter 2, Teacher as a Manager of the Classroom, provides *positive strategies and innovative systems for creating rules and procedures that support learning goals.* It offers suggestions for establishing procedures that promote positive behavior in whole-class, small-group, and individual learning situations. Intervention strategies for dealing with difficult student behaviors are also discussed.

• Chapter 3, Teacher as a Designer of Instruction, offers *guidelines for designing curriculum and instruction* that meet high standards and reach all learners. This chapter is guided by the question, what do my students need to learn? It helps teachers navigate the challenging process of determining standards, designing lesson plans, and developing units.

• Chapter 4, Teacher as an Assessor, answers the question, *how do I know my students are learning?* The chapter describes how you can effectively examine student understanding through a broad range of assessments. It highlights ways to use effective measures before, during, and after the instructional process and provides specific examples.

• Chapter 5, Teacher as a Promoter of Literacy, examines *ways you can offer a systematic and balanced instructional approach to literacy* that ensures student success. This chapter also discusses the importance of developing a strong independent reading program and gives suggestions for building an excellent classroom library. The chapter also includes a glossary of current literacy terms.

• Chapter 6, Teacher as a Facilitator and Guide for Learning, gives you *a wide range of effective and proven teaching strategies that facilitate learning.* This chapter provides information on strategies such as cooperative learning, Socratic questioning, and cross-age tutoring.

• Chapter 7, Teacher as a Relationship Builder, examines the various relationships encountered in teaching and provides *ideas for connecting effectively with students and parents*. The chapter offers ideas and activities for deepening connections with students, dealing productively with difficult students, and communicating with parents, as well as practical strategies for confronting "energy bandits" and caring for oneself.

• Chapter 8, Teacher as a Communicator, gives *suggestions and strategies for oral and written communications with parents and colleagues*. It offers tips on how to make parent conferences successful as well as ideas for making back-to-school nights informative and interesting. Tips for creating newsletters and Web sites and using e-mail are also included.

• Chapter 9, Teacher as a Learner, highlights *the importance of teachers' becoming lifelong learners*. It offers many suggestions for keeping the educational fire lit. The chapter demonstrates that teaching is a far richer experience when it is done in collaboration with others and when it focuses on continually improving teaching practice. The chapter describes the many vehicles that offer support and opportunity to grow as a teacher.

Each chapter offers powerful, specific suggestions within each role that can make your first few years of teaching effective and successful. The goal is not to overwhelm you with "to do" lists but to offer you plenty of support and options as you develop in your practice. Each chapter includes Web site recommendations (Worthwhile Web Sites), connections to brain research (Brain Bits), and advice for the first days or weeks of school (First Week Flags). In addition, reflection questions are included at the end of each chapter to give you some direction as you evaluate your own practice. In fact, if you use this book during your induction program, you may engage in these reflections with others who are new to teaching.

You are embarking on the career of a lifetime. May your journey be filled with many moments of the satisfaction of a job well done, emotions that touch your soul, and the knowledge that no other job in the world is better than teaching.

Teacher as a Creator of Classroom Environment

"HOW CAN I DESIGN MY CLASSROOM TO MAXIMIZE STUDENT LEARNING?"

Remember the feeling you had when you walked into your school for the first time? The principal welcomed you aboard and handed you the key. You walked to your classroom and slowly opened the door. The lights were off, and the room was eerily silent. You probably felt overwhelmed with excitement, fear, and peace. As you surveyed the classroom, you realized that within this room you and your students would share learning experiences over the year. You had arrived at your new home, your home away from home, your classroom.

During the year, you will spend a lot of time in your classroom. In fact, many times during the year you will feel as though you spend more time in your classroom than you do at home.

Through your design, your classroom can become more than just a room with four walls. You can transform your classroom into an environment that encourages, entices, and celebrates learning. Your classroom can become a reflection of your soul; it can be as unique as your own DNA.

This chapter provides you not only with ideas for personalizing your classroom to reflect your style but also with tips for creating an environment that will make your job easier and optimize your students' learning. Your classroom environment has a significant impact on the teaching and learning process. By optimally designing and arranging your classroom environment, you can do the following:

- Promote attentiveness and engagement in the learning process
- Facilitate positive social interaction among students
- Decrease the likelihood that students will engage in challenging behaviors
- Provide powerful opportunities for whole-group, small-group, and individual instruction
- Foster students' independence and feelings of empowerment in regard to their learning
- Boost opportunities for practicing and generalizing skills across different types of activities and settings
- Increase student achievement

■ DESIGNING YOUR CLASSROOM ENVIRONMENT

The classroom environment is too important to be taken lightly. Yet no two classrooms are exactly the same. The room arrangement, bulletin boards, furniture, art, and lighting all directly reflect you. Be sure to consider these two questions when designing your classroom:

- What is the best classroom environment for promoting student learning and facilitating positive classroom interactions?
- What is the best arrangement and room decor for me personally?

All teachers need a classroom that makes them feel happy, comfortable, and inspired when they walk in each morning. It takes time and experimentation to create the best environment. As you design your classroom, keep the following suggestions in mind:

- *Establish a climate of learning right from the start.* Design bulletin boards and arrange furniture to promote learning. Your classroom environment should proclaim, "This is a serious learning environment!"

Avoid overdoing your decorations.

- *Fight the temptation to overdecorate your classroom, because too much decoration can distract you and your students.* You may add and subtract decorations as you go, but avoid overdoing your decorations. Remember, it is more important to concentrate on your teaching than to stay late to make your classroom look gorgeous.

Finding Your Own Design Style

There is no single right way to organize a classroom. One quick avenue to frustration is to compare your room with that of last year's Teacher of the Year. When you begin, use your adventurous spirit. Remember that nothing in your classroom is set in cement. If you don't like an arrangement, change it. Redo the bulletin board even though you put it up just last week. Keep experimenting until your spirit yells out, "Yes, this works for me and my students!"

Designing Your Classroom Environment

The first years of teaching are all about finding your own unique style in your classroom arrangement and decor. For some, this comes naturally. These teachers walk into their first classroom and within a month or so have it organized and beautiful. For others, finding a personal style is more challenging. Use the following five-step plan to get started:

1. *Make a list of items that have captured your attention in other teachers' classrooms* (e.g., nooks, comfy pillows, bright colors, seating arrangements, learning centers).

2. *Sketch a layout that might work in your classroom.* Sketch on graph paper before you start arranging and decorating.

3. *Evaluate your design and decor ideas through an interior decorator's perspective.* (More information on how to do this appears later in this chapter.)

4. *Arrange the room.* Sit in different seats throughout the room to ensure that all students can see the front of the room and have enough space.

5. *Try the arrangement with your students.* See if you and the students like the arrangement. If students are stumbling over one another or struggling to see the board or complaining about space, adjust the arrangement. If the arrangement seems to work, take time to work on the smaller details and make minor adjustments so that the classroom works even better.

Arranging the Room to Facilitate Positive Classroom Interactions

The way you arrange the furniture in your classroom will play a critical role in helping students interact positively with you and each other. It is imperative that you consider how to arrange your room so that you create an orderly learning environment. Poorly arranged classrooms—where students seem to be sitting almost on top of each other and where disorder reigns—promote tense, unfocused, and negative interactions among students. Students feel they must fight for their own space and belongings. They feel frustrated by not having an orderly environment to call their own. In contrast, deftly arranged classrooms—where students have their own space and where order prevails—promote positive student interactions. Students relish the order and space provided through well-designed learning centers, private nooks, and small-group meeting areas.

> It is imperative that you consider how to arrange your room so that you create an orderly learning environment.

Guiding Questions for Determining Room Arrangement

Arranging and rearranging furniture requires planning and elbow grease. Begin by taking an inventory of the furniture in the room. Report broken furniture to the custodian and administrator as soon as possible so it can be fixed or replaced. Next, take time to consider possible room arrangements. Use the following questions to help you plan your arrangement:

- How can I arrange the students' seats to ensure that all students can easily see the front of the classroom?
- Where will I put my classroom library?
- Where might I meet with small groups of students or individual students?
- Where will I place materials so students have access to them? (Materials might include pens, marking pens, paper, crayons, etc.)
- Will I have any learning centers? Where will I put them?
- What areas will be designated quiet areas? What areas will be designated active areas (where students know they can interact with one another)?
- Where will my clear and safe traffic paths be? How will I promote safe traffic flow?
- Where will I place my classroom computers?
- What kind of storage do I need?
- Does this arrangement lend itself to maintaining order?
- Does this arrangement have balance or symmetry? (For more information on balance and symmetry, see the "Interior Design Principles" section later in this chapter.)
- Are there safety or fire codes I need to know about, and how can I find this information?

Several sample classroom layouts are shown in Figures 1.1 through 1.4. You may choose one of these layouts and adapt it to suit your classroom needs. Or you may experiment with each layout before settling on one or two favorites. Of course, the size and shape of your classroom and your furniture will dictate what you can and cannot do with your layout.

Keep two key factors in mind as you determine your final layout: You must be able to monitor the room easily, and you must be able to maneuver from one side of the classroom to another quickly. Ideally, you should have a clear, short pathway that allows you to easily walk around the room and monitor students working at their desks or group tables. If you have to climb over objects, duck around furniture, and slither between desks to get to a student in the back row, then you must modify your arrangement.

Take time to examine the layouts used by teachers in your school. Veteran teachers who are teaching the same course or the same grade may give you some advice about how to arrange your classroom. While you may discover several good ideas, remember: The arrangement must work for you and your students.

> **Take time to examine the layouts used by teachers in your school.**

Each layout has advantages and disadvantages (see Table 1.1). Consider the (traditional) horizontal row layout, in which all the desks are lined up and face the board. Some teachers will tell you that you should never use this arrangement because they believe it is not conducive to teaching and learning. However, some teachers continue to use this arrangement and find it effective. Use whatever arrangement works best for you and your students. Choose a layout based on your students' learning needs. You may begin the school year by using the horizontal arrangement because you feel you need to gain control of your class and feel that students need more structure. As the year progresses, you may adapt the layout to a cooperative arrangement. Some years you may start off using the cooperative learning arrangement.

Figure 1.1 Sample Classroom Layout: Straight Horizontal Rows

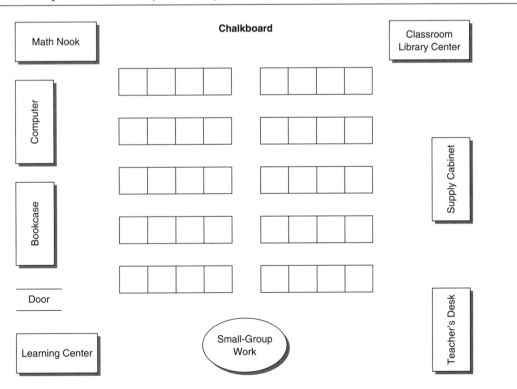

Figure 1.2   Sample Classroom Layout: Double E

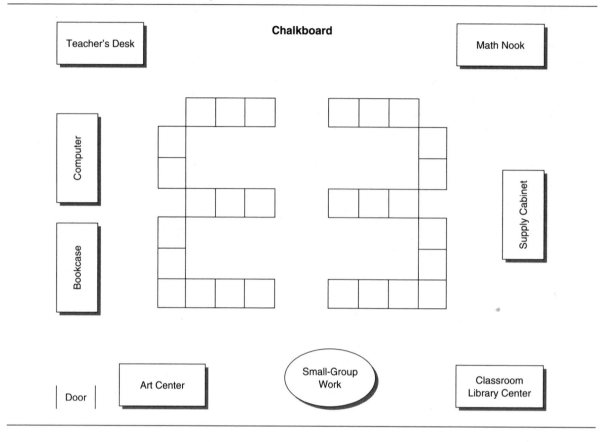

Figure 1.3   Sample Classroom Layout: U Shape

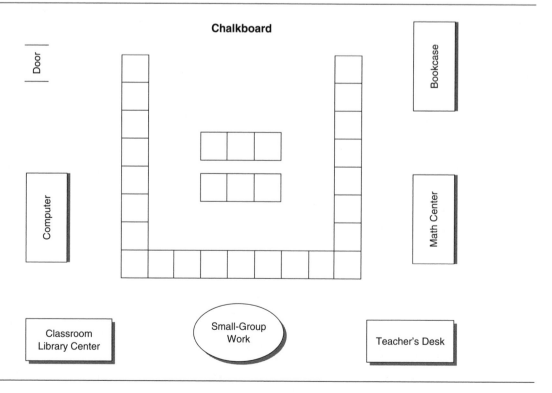

Figure 1.4   Sample Classroom Layout: Cooperative Learning

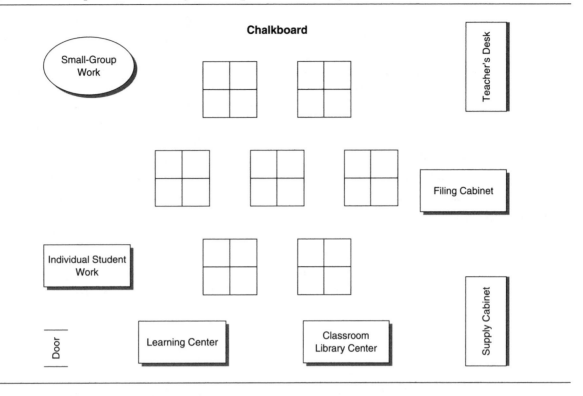

Table 1.1   Advantages and Disadvantages of Classroom Layouts

Layout	Advantages	Disadvantages
Straight horizontal rows	Provides more structure (for students who need structure) and less peer interaction.	Hinders communication during small-group work and doesn't provide much open space in the classroom.
Double E	Provides students with an environment for working closely with peers without seating students across from one another.	Reduces the amount of space for walking through the classroom (depending on classroom size).
U shape	Provides students with a good view of the front of the classroom and teacher.	Makes some students in the back of the room feel far away from the action.
Cooperative learning	Provides opportunities for students to work together throughout the day and allows for teamwork and socialization.	Provides ample (and sometimes too many) opportunities for students to talk to one another throughout the day.

Changing Seating Assignments or Rearranging the Room

How often you change students' seating assignments or rearrange the room is dependent on your preferences and your students' needs. Some teachers change students' seats each month or several times during the year to keep things fresh. It is up to you to decide how much time and energy you wish to spend on developing new seating charts and room arrangements. However, be sure to keep the following ideas in mind:

> **Never change the seating arrangement immediately before a unit assessment or standardized test.**

• *Never change the seating arrangement immediately before a unit assessment or standardized test.* Changing students' seats hinders their memory process. The upheaval caused by the change is not conducive to strong performance on tests.

• *Always maintain an updated seating chart.* (Sketch a chart, using boxes to indicate each seat, and write the students' names in the boxes.) A seating chart is especially important when you are absent and another teacher must take over your class. Keep this seating chart where it is easy to find—either on top of or in the top drawer of your desk.

Beyond Basic Design: Looking at Learning Centers

Learning centers are areas where an individual or a group of students can work on a specific project or assignment. These centers offer students the time and space to work on powerful learning activities, to stretch out and read books, or to create art projects.

Tips for Designing Learning Centers

• *Select a location away from normal student activity.* This way, students working at the center won't be interrupted by students walking by.

• *Arrange the furniture to give the center a feeling of privacy.* You might simply turn a table away from the main classroom area so that it faces a wall, or you might move a bookshelf to create a nook. If you design for privacy, students will feel as if they have a separate location in which to work.

• *Enhance your reading center with bookcases full of books that welcome students into the center.* Provide pillows or carpet remnants for students to use while sitting or lying on the floor to read.

• *Outline the learning activity clearly.* Post directions on the wall students are facing.

• *Describe the center activity to the entire class before students use the learning center.* Remind students that working in a learning center is a privilege and that if they goof around, they will forfeit this privilege for a while.

What Do I Really Need in My Classroom to Get Started?

Having certain equipment and other items in your classroom can make your life easier from the start. If you cannot obtain the materials listed below before school begins or within the first week of school, make it your goal to get them. Having these materials will send you down the right path toward designing a great classroom environment.

- Overhead projector (Be prepared. Know where to find spare bulbs and how to change the light. Invariably, the overhead bulb will blow during a formal observation or a wonderful learning moment. Also, be sure to obtain transparencies and marking pens.)
- Polaroid or digital camera (Be sure to have extra film for the Polaroid camera. Use the camera to capture special moments in the classroom or to take pictures of students at the beginning of the year for a bulletin board display.)
- Moveable cart or cabinet (Place the overhead projector on the cart or cabinet. Be sure the cart or cabinet also has ample room to store and transport materials.)
- Extra chairs (for centers and other group work)
- Stool (Place the stool at the front of the classroom. Use it to give your feet a quick rest while still maintaining eye contact with the class.)
- Wall-mounted projector screen
- World map, national map, and globe
- Precut letters in a variety of sizes and colors (Use the letters on bulletin boards throughout the year.)
- Plastic washtubs (Use the tubs to store art projects, workbooks, and other items. Clearly label the tubs to help students know what is in them.)
- Three-hole punch
- Tray or small box of usable scrap paper
- Boxes of tissues
- Yardstick or meter stick
- Lost-and-found container

Your Teacher Space

Many teachers need and want to have a sacred space, their own space. Most teachers consider their desk and the corner the desk occupies as their own space. Some classrooms include alcoves for the teacher's desk, bookcase, and filing cabinet. Within the space, teachers may post pictures of their loved ones, certificates, or artwork that is meaningful to them. However, some teachers do not carve out a sacred space for themselves. They allow students to use the teacher's desk to make up tests or to read silently. Students may walk up to the teacher's desk and help themselves to pens and pencils. Students may feel that the teacher's desk is community space.

Whether you choose to have a sacred space or not, be sure students are well aware of your expectations and rules when it comes to your desk. Remember, classroom discipline problems are directly related to the distance between the teacher and the student. The closer the teacher can be to the students, the fewer the problems.

Designing Your Teacher Space

Classroom discipline problems are directly related to the distance between the teacher and the student.

As a teacher, you will notice right away that your days are filled with a lot of moving, walking, and general activity. Yet it is important for you to have a space of your own in your classroom. Your space should include a well-organized desk, a file cabinet, and a safe place for your personal belongings. You may not have a lot of time during the day to sit at your desk, but having your own space for those long hours you put in before and after school will help you keep yourself organized and on track. Here are a few suggestions for designing your own space:

• *Place your desk facing the students so that in those rare moments when you sit at your desk during the day, you can easily monitor everything going on in the classroom.* The best place to position your desk is in the corner farthest away from the door and facing the room. This way, you can always see who is coming in and going out of the room.

• *Have a secure location in your area for your purse, keys, and other personal items.*

• *Make sure you have a comfortable chair.* Those long before- and after-school hours of grading papers and catching up on other work will be greatly enhanced by a comfortable chair.

• *Keep a stacking tray on top of your desk to keep worksheets, notices, newsletters, and other files handy and accessible.*

• *Have one of your drawers be a file drawer where you can keep student files, long-range plans, checklists, emergency procedures, school and district policies, correspondence from parents, an emergency substitutes plan, and other paperwork.* You may want another file drawer for curriculum units, divided by subject areas.

• *Have these items within easy reach: a nice pair of adult scissors, a glue stick, correction fluid, highlighters, paper clips, a calculator, pens, felt pens, overhead pens, a ruler, pencils, and sticky notes.* You may want to have pencils in unusual colors (such as bright orange or blue) so that when a student borrows one, you will be able to retrieve it easily.

Using Bulletin Board Designs to Help in Teaching and Learning

Effective teachers use bulletin boards for purposes beyond simply displaying student work. Different types of bulletin boards can be used for different reasons:

• *A procedures bulletin board* includes schedules, procedures, classroom jobs, emergency information, menus, birthdays, and other such information. Students can independently refer to the board without having to rely on or interrupt you for information.

• *A bulletin board of model student work* includes work you want students to emulate. You may display what a well-written five-paragraph essay or a neat math paper looks like. Make a point to explain why each piece was selected. Consciously vary which students' work and what type of work you choose to display on the board.

• *A current events bulletin board* features important world events. Due to time constraints, many teachers must curtail the amount of time they can spend discussing current events. These teachers briefly discuss world events each week and post articles and pictures for students to read and look at during their free time.

• *A curriculum-based bulletin board* displays information about a curriculum-based unit, related student work, and additional information applicable to the specific topic of study.

A bulletin board can also be used to display student artwork. However, it is important to remember that a bulletin board is a valuable space and should be used for a specific purpose. As a new teacher, you need not worry about making your classroom look beautiful. Instead, you should concentrate on making every inch of your classroom work to your overall goal: creating independent, well-behaved, and motivated learners.

Bulletin Board Tips

➤ *Purchase professionally created borders.* Borders enhance the appearance of your bulletin boards. You may also purchase precut letters in various colors to use on your bulletin boards.

➤ *Remove background paper before it fades.* Change the background paper occasionally to freshen up the look of your bulletin boards.

➤ *If you run out of bulletin board space, use reusable adhesive to hang work on blank walls.* You can purchase reusable adhesives such as Sticky Tack® in most hardware or department stores.

Using the Power of Lighting in Your Classroom

You cannot control the amount of natural light present in your classroom. You may have a classroom with a wide swath of windows or a classroom that doesn't have any windows. It is up to you to do your best with what you are given.

We know from recent studies by Tim Berman and others that natural light increases students' academic achievement levels. One study tracked students in classrooms with very little or no natural light and compared them with a similar group of students in classrooms that had windows and skylights. The students in classrooms

Students in classrooms with more natural light outperformed the students with less.

with more natural light outperformed the students with less. With these studies in mind, teachers should seek to optimize the lighting in their classrooms. The following suggestions will help you maximize the light in your room and use the light you have to the best advantage:

• Refrain from blocking the light that comes through the windows. Don't cover windows with heavy drapes or an overabundance of student work. However, be sure to have a way to darken the room during certain activities (e.g., movies and demonstrations).

- Keep windows clean.

- Place a learning center, reading nook, or small-group center by the window if possible.

┌─ **Worthwhile Web Sites** ─────────┐

Here are two Web sites that offer some tips for classroom arrangements and decor:

Peak Learning
(www.peaklearn.com/article.asp?A_ID=14)

Writing Lesson Plans: Seating Arrangements
(www.huntington.edu/education/lessonplanning/
seating.html)

└────────────────────────────────────┘

- If your room lacks natural light, purchase inexpensive lamps and place them around the room. (Check with your administrator to be sure the lights adhere to fire regulations.)

- Be aware of students whose visual needs require more or less light. For example, some students may be extremely light sensitive and should be seated with their backs to the window.

■ INTERIOR DESIGN PRINCIPLES TO HELP YOU CREATE THE CLASSROOM OF YOUR DREAMS

Once you have designed a layout that you feel creates a warm, positive classroom environment, step back and look at your design through the eyes of an interior designer. Designers follow three basic principles when decorating an interior space: order, symmetry, and balance. Teachers can use these same principles when designing their classrooms. The following descriptions explain how you can use each principle to create the classroom of your dreams.

Order

Order is the logical arrangement of separate elements within a space. Order happens when you stack books in a bookcase, organize writing materials (pencils, pens, and crayons) in the supply cupboard, and arrange desks so that it is easy to walk between them. Maintaining classroom order is essential for promoting successful teaching experiences. Without order, you will find yourself immersed in chaos, feeling scattered and unfocused. If you cannot find the items you need, if you are constantly tripping over students' belongings, and if you often lose keys under a stack of papers, your classroom experiences will be frustrating and ineffective.

> Maintaining classroom order is essential for promoting successful teaching experiences.

One of the most important points of this chapter is that your classroom environment must help, not hinder, your teaching. Your teaching life is busy and full, but your work surroundings should be simple and uncluttered.

Establishing and maintaining order in a classroom is one of the most challenging aspects of managing a classroom environment. However, when you realize that order is an important component in the classroom environment, you will mount a daily battle against disorder. If you are consistent and if you work on order a little bit at a time, you will be rewarded with an orderly and organized classroom. Here are some effective suggestions to help you along this path:

• *Find a home for frequently used items.* For example, place scratch paper on the second shelf of the cupboard and store marking pens in a tub on the third shelf. Make students aware of the homes for each item. Explain that every item has a home. Remind students (more than once) where certain items go. The quicker students know that each item has a home, the better they will be at maintaining order. Do not move items unless you make everyone aware of the move.

• *After you've established homes for each item, label shelves to help students identify where to place things—for example, dictionaries, nonfiction books, and fiction books.* When appropriate, use containers to hold items and clearly label each container. Labels help students remember where to place items when asked to put them away. Take advantage of all the wonderful colors available in the office supply store. Instead of manila folders, use bright purple and red folders. Look for file boxes in cheery colors.

• *Use sticky notes in special colors to help you remember certain things.* For example, you could use blue sticky notes for student notes, green sticky notes for parent issues, and orange sticky notes for lesson ideas.

• *Clear away clutter and arrange desks to create an unobstructed traffic flow around the classroom.* It is critical that your classroom have ample passageways throughout the room so students don't find themselves bumping into one another and you don't need to hurdle backpacks to get to a student in need of help.

• *Give each piece of furniture its needed space.* Overcrowding is unsettling to students and teachers. Give students (and their belongings) ample personal space. You may be surprised how much a little extra space improves students' attitudes and decreases their misbehavior.

• *Tell students your expectations for maintaining order at and around their desks.* Set aside one afternoon per week for cleanup. Spend the last 30 minutes of the week having students organize their belongings and clean the classroom work areas.

• *Once a week, after the students have left the room, dedicate a few minutes to cleaning and organizing.* Clean out cupboards and organize materials.

Symmetry

Symmetry is the exact correspondence of forms and shapes on opposite sides of an imaginary dividing line. Symmetry is all around us. Look at the moon, a piece of notebook paper, a bridge, or a basketball, and you will see symmetry. Any of these items can be divided in half and folded perfectly together.

Probably the greatest use of symmetry in the classroom is the arrangement of student desks. Teachers naturally use symmetry in their classroom arrangements. You may place 20 desks in four rows of 5, thereby creating a symmetrical arrangement. If you drew an imaginary line down the middle of the classroom, the desks on one side would be symmetrical to the desks on the other side. On the other hand, you would not jam 15 student desks into one area of the room and leave the other 5 desks in another area. Such asymmetry would be visually unsettling.

Train yourself to be aware of symmetry in smaller, subtler areas in your classroom. Check your bulletin boards and the objects you've placed on your bookshelves and tables. Be aware of symmetry in these details.

Symmetry brings a sense of peace and serenity to an environment. Use symmetry whenever possible in desk arrangements, bulletin board designs, bookshelves, learning centers, and other small areas of the room. Our eyes are naturally attracted to symmetrical things.

> **Symmetry brings a sense of peace and serenity to an environment.**

Balance

Balance is similar to symmetry. While symmetry requires parts to be exactly alike, balance only requires items to be equally distributed or harmoniously arranged. Balance can be achieved by contrasting two elements, such as light and dark. Balance requires that two sides appear to be evenly weighted, but the sides need not exactly mirror one another.

Our eyes desire this illusion of equilibrium. We are very aware when a room or any part of the room is not in balance. If we enter a classroom where the walls and bulletin boards feature only bright yellows, oranges, and reds, we will sense that the room needs some darker colors to balance the vibrant colors. Another example of balance is placing a bookcase on one side of the chalkboard (or white board) and a table (or other piece of furniture) on the other side. When students look at this arrangement, their eyes immediately recognize that the room is balanced.

The key to balance is being aware of the vertical lines in your classroom. When you create a learning center in the corner of a room, think of the meeting place of two walls as a vertical line. Then as you design the center, use the line to balance the placement of tables, chairs, pillows, bookcases, and other items.

■ KEEPING THE CREATIVE JUICES FLOWING

You can use several time-tested techniques to come up with fresh ideas for arranging your classroom. These techniques, described below, should help you keep your creative juices flowing throughout the year.

Nosy Neighbor Technique

Become a "nosy neighbor": Observe how other teachers arrange and decorate their classrooms. Notice what you like and don't like. Be observant when you sit and talk to your colleagues in their classrooms. Take time to look around their rooms and notice their small touches. Everyone has a unique style, but sometimes seeing someone else's ideas helps you define your own style.

Different Perspectives Technique

Take time to view your classroom from different perspectives. Looking at the room from various angles will open up a world of new ideas. Sit in various spots around your room—the reading center, the math nook, students' desks at the front and back of the room. Notice subtle things such as the lighting; the view of the chalkboard (or white board); the appearance of the bulletin boards and posters; and the order, symmetry, and balance of the furniture. Allow your mind to roam the room looking for things that might need to be changed or redone, and write them all down. When you have extra time, revisit your list and begin to make changes.

Open Space Technique

Another way to recharge your decorator's eye is to be aware of the hazards of clutter. Some people need to see space and emptiness in order to create and design. Take time to clear out clutter. Empty that big bin of papers sitting on top of the bookcase and get rid of that small table that you fought so hard to get but never really use. We teachers are natural collectors and pack rats, so sometimes it is scary for us to get rid of things. However, if you do not have open spaces and breathing room in your classroom, you will not have the energy to design the classroom you desire.

> ## Brain Bits
>
> The 1990s were called the "decade of the brain" because of the overwhelming amount of research done on the brain. Researchers such as Ron Brandt (1998b), Renate and Geoffrey Caine (1991), Marian Diamond (1988), and Pat Wolfe (2001) have led the way in helping educators learn how the brain functions. These researchers discovered that enriched environments positively affect brain stimulation and growth. A study from the Salk Institute (Gage, 1997) showed that aging mice who lived in a stimulating and enriched environment produced three times the number of new brain cells as mice did who lived in a nonstimulating environment. Several components contribute to an enriched environment; many are covered in this book. One component is the physical environment that students inhabit each day. By making your room a bright, stimulating, and challenging place, you will actually encourage students' brains to grow more brain cells. Environmental factors in addition to the physical environment affect students' achievement. These include classrooms that promote the development of a wide range of skills and interests, stimulate different senses at different times, present varied and challenging activities for students, provide regular feedback to students, and create a stress-free atmosphere, all of which allow students to be active participants in learning rather than passive observers.

Techniques That Use the Talent (and Time) of Others

Parent volunteers are always looking for ways to assist in the classroom. If you feel overwhelmed by the thought of creating another bulletin board or if you are running out of ideas for organizing your room, enlist the help of parent volunteers. You may discover that one (or more) of the parents is an artist!

Your students are another resource for talent. By asking students for help, you will not only get great ideas for freshening and reorganizing your room; you will also give students an opportunity to shine. This strategy is especially powerful with students who might struggle academically but are great with hands-on activities.

A LAST LOOK AT THE TEACHER ■
AS A CREATOR OF CLASSROOM ENVIRONMENT

This chapter discussed many different elements to consider while designing a classroom environment. Use the classroom arrangement checklist in Figure 1.5 to remind you of these elements. Classroom arrangement— from seating arrangements to bulletin boards—is a very important part of a successful and efficient classroom. Remember to ask yourself this guiding question as you make decisions about your classroom environment: Does this (furniture arrangement, bulletin board, lighting, etc.) promote student learning? If you look at any item or design feature in the classroom and find that it has very little to do with student learning, then you know a change is due. Everything in a classroom can be used to promote student learning. If you follow this guiding principle, you will have an outstanding classroom environment that will make your job easier and more successful.

Figure 1.5   Classroom Arrangement Checklist

Door

❑ Area around door is uncluttered and easy to access.

❑ There is enough space inside the door for lining up students.

❑ Inside of door is free of work or papers that can fall off or hinder access.

Walls

❑ Displays are at students' eye level.

❑ Bulletin boards offer classroom information, instruction, and models for student work.

❑ Posted schedules and information are current and easy for students to find.

❑ Open wall space is provided for a visual break.

❑ Malfunctioning outlets or blemished walls have been reported for repair.

❑ Balance, order, and symmetry are used in visual displays.

Furniture

❑ Students' desks are the appropriate size and are in good condition.

❑ Each student has an assigned seat.

❑ Each student is required to keep desk area organized and neat.

❑ Desks are arranged so each student can see the board easily and can participate in class discussions.

❑ Areas in the classroom (e.g., classroom library, computer center, learning centers, instructional materials) are clearly designated.

Equipment and Materials

❑ Materials and equipment are stored properly; they are easily accessible and kept in the areas where they are used.

❑ Materials and equipment are inventoried regularly.

❑ Students are aware of where and when they can access materials and equipment.

Comfort

❑ Temperature control is adequate.

❑ Lighting is used to enhance learning objectives. In most cases, more light is better than less light.

Questions for Reflection

How can I arrange my classroom so that it is more helpful to me and promotes student learning?

_____

_____

_____

_____

_____

_____

What small changes can I make in the classroom environment to freshen up my room?

_____

_____

_____

_____

_____

_____

Where do I need to reestablish order in my classroom?

_____

_____

_____

_____

_____

_____

Teacher as a Manager of the Classroom

(Continued)

"HOW DO I CREATE A CLASSROOM THAT RUNS SMOOTHLY?"

Think back to your own education and try to remember the classes in which you had wonderful learning experiences. Perhaps it was your third-grade class or your high school mathematics class. What do you think made the difference between these classes and others?

Chances are that the teachers of your favorite classes were masters, not only of the content they taught, but also of the overall management of their classroom. In addition to making the content interesting and relevant, your teacher most likely made sure that things ran smoothly and efficiently. He or she made your learning a priority and structured the classroom based on that priority. If clear expectations for classroom behavior had not been established, or if the management of the environment had not been effective, the amount of learning you achieved in these classes would have been drastically reduced.

As you may have experienced firsthand, there are some content experts whose classroom teaching is less than effective because they lack management skills. Clearly, knowing subject matter is important, but the overall success of all teachers depends on their ability to anticipate, plan, and respond to events that occur throughout the day. As a beginning teacher, your mission is to realize both aspects of teaching: content *and* management. You must create an effective learning environment through which you can deliver meaningful content instruction.

■ FIRST IMPRESSIONS

Within the first 15 minutes of a new school year or semester, students develop an impression about who you are and about what type of learning experience you will offer them. You can proactively prevent management difficulties and set the stage for a successful classroom experience by thoughtfully planning and establishing a structure from the beginning. This signals to students that you have prioritized their learning.

As you can probably guess, your students do not enter your classroom with a clear understanding of your expectations and management procedures. Students need to learn your rules, routines, and procedures within the first several days or weeks of school. During these days or weeks, thread your lessons with clarification, instruction, and practice of the rules, routines, and procedures. By doing so, you establish a classroom management system, and you increase students' awareness and ability to function within the classroom structure. Through this ongoing development of structure, students become familiar with your teaching style, your expectations for behavior, and the procedures they must follow to complete the simplest of tasks.

KNOW YOUR TEACHING CONTEXT ■

Before you can design an effective classroom management plan, you must understand your teaching situation, your students, and your school. The minute you sign your contract, begin seeking answers to the following questions:

- Who are my students?
- What is my class size?
- What is the schedule of the school (including recess, transitions between class periods, lunches, etc.)?
- What is the educational background of my students? Is this their first year in a new setting? Is there a high rate of transience?
- What are some of the students' interests?
- What information is available on my students through their school files? (See First Week Flag.)
- What are the rules and policies of the school?
- What is the culture of the community?
- What subjects am I expected to teach?

Brain Bits

By nature, individuals are wired to seek new information, and students are wired to look for connections, predictable patterns, and expectations in the classroom. They seek predictability and structure in their environment. When you provide a well-organized management system within your classroom, students can more easily attend to the important task of learning (Wolfe, 2001).

First Week Flag

Cumulative Files

As a teacher, you have access to the educational records of your students. These cumulative files (commonly called *cume* files) serve as historical records of students' school experiences, background information, achievements, and testing results. Cumulative files are confidential and are kept in locked file cabinets in the school office. You are obligated to keep their information confidential, and you must use the information for educational purposes only. Be sure to check on your school's policies and procedures for accessing student files.

■ ON THE ROAD TO A WELL-MANAGED CLASSROOM

Begin by setting management objectives. Determine what your goals are for the classroom. You may adapt and extend schoolwide goals, or you may create your own goals by following another process. Your management objectives should answer these questions: What procedures will ensure that my students are able to get the most out of learning? What systems will help me provide effective instruction?

When developing a classroom management strategy, we often think in terms of encouraging students to do things. This leads us to focus on control rather than on learning. Effective teachers know that the most effective classroom management programs keep learning at the forefront. Design your management goals with the focus on learning. Figure 2.1 shows three simple management goals that focus on learning.

Figure 2.1   Three Simple Management Goals That Focus on Learning

❏ Establish and protect a productive and organized learning environment.
❏ Provide an environment that fosters respect, independence, safety, and acceptance of all students.
❏ Ensure that all students meet the learning standards.

Obviously, merely establishing these goals is not enough. If you wish to create a smoothly running classroom, you must also ask yourself questions such as, What would it look like if my instructional time were protected? What actions would eliminate interruptions? How would my students interact if they were in an environment conducive to social skills development? These questions help you identify what you will see when you accomplish your goals and what actions you can take to achieve your major goals. Use your answers to develop a list of critical rules, routines, and procedures (see Table 2.1). By identifying what you should see when you have accomplished your goals, you not only establish the foundation for developing classroom rules and routines; you also set the foundation for the design and delivery of your instruction.

Establishing Classroom Rules

There are two schools of thought when it comes to developing classroom rules. One school (Jonson, 2002) supports the idea that teachers and students together should develop rules and procedures, while the other school (Canter & Associates, 1998) maintains that teachers alone should determine class rules. Both methods are acceptable. However, you must ask yourself a few questions before choosing which method to use:

- What is my level of experience?
- Do I have a clear idea of what my targeted rules might be?
- Am I comfortable facilitating a dialogue among my students that will yield the results I want?

Again, either method is acceptable, and the choice is not an all-or-nothing proposition. You may even opt for a hybrid approach: developing your rules and asking students for feedback or edits.

Whichever approach you choose, take time, before students enter your classroom for the first time, to ponder and list all the routines and rules you want them to know. Many schools and districts require parents and students to read and acknowledge district- or schoolwide behavior guidelines. Check to see whether these guidelines exist. If they do, use them as a basis for your classroom behavior guidelines.

> **Before students enter your classroom for the first time, ponder and list all the routines and rules you want them to know.**

Table 2.1   Translating Classroom Goals Into Actions

Goal	What Does It Look Like?
Establish and protect a productive and organized learning environment.	• Students come to class ready to learn and prepared with materials. • Students are actively engaged in learning activities with minimal downtime. • Transitions are planned and smoothly implemented with minimal confusion and loss of time. • Students follow procedures to get their needs met without interrupting the rest of the class. • The school and class are committed to reducing or eliminating interruptions during instructional time.
Provide an environment that fosters respect, independence, safety, and acceptance of all students.	• Students' abilities increase so they can do more tasks with less assistance by the end of the year. • Students understand the rules, routines, and procedures that communicate the teacher's expectations for their learning and behavior. • Students work collaboratively, using respectful communication and actions. • Students demonstrate respect for different opinions, backgrounds, and abilities.
Ensure that all students meet the learning standards.	• Activities are linked to specific learning goals. • Lessons are organized around the standards. • The learning environment is set up to accommodate all types of learners. • Instructional strategies reflect a variety of techniques in order to reach all students.

Rights, Responsibilities, Privileges

Prior to developing or reviewing classroom rules with students, introduce and discuss the concepts of students' rights, responsibilities, and privileges. Use a carousel activity to introduce the concepts. This activity works especially well with older students and may even address key standards found within your curriculum.

Hang three pieces of chart paper around the room. Label the first paper *Rights*, the second paper *Responsibilities*, and the third paper *Privileges.* Divide your class into three groups. Ask each group to start at one of the papers. Instruct groups to spend 5 minutes brainstorming ideas for their category. When 5 minutes have passed, ask groups to rotate to the next paper and add ideas to it. When another 5 minutes have passed, ask the groups to rotate and brainstorm again. In merely 15 minutes, the students will have created an advance organizer for the rules and procedures they will design for your classroom.

Carousel

A carousel is a great cooperative strategy that can be adapted to a variety of instructional purposes (Johnson, Johnson, & Holubec, 1994). In carousel activities, small groups of students travel to various stations, where they participate in brainstorming or problem-solving activities. The stations provide students with opportunities to be actively engaged in working collaboratively with their peers.

You can create a carousel by dividing a topic into various categories. For example, if you are discussing weather, you can use these categories: *Earth's atmosphere, clouds, humidity, causes of weather,* and *weather forecasting.* Create a station for each category and provide paper and marking pens at each station. Then divide the class into five groups and ask each group to start at one of the stations. Ask groups to list all the information they know about their category. Allow 5–10 minutes (or whatever amount of time is appropriate) at the first station. Then ask the groups to rotate (as if they were riding a carousel) to the next station and follow the same procedure they used at the first station. Continue rotating groups until they have visited all five stations. Once each group has visited all the stations, the students will have compiled a great deal of information.

You can use carousels at the beginning of the lesson to activate prior knowledge or at the end of a unit to review information. You may type up the information that students have brainstormed and give it to students to use as a review sheet.

Keep in mind that your students are going to test you on these rules, so you must be sure that the rules you develop are truly important to you and that you can consistently apply them. Your students will quickly get the message that you mean business when it is clear that you do not bend on certain rules. If you clarify the connection between the classroom environment and students' ability to learn, students will understand that your expectations for appropriate behavior are intended to benefit rather than control them.

When developing your rules, always reference the overall goals you created earlier (Figure 2.1). In addition, ask yourself whether they meet the three E's: *Essential, Enforceable,* and *Effective* (see Figure 2.2). Use the three E's to evaluate the rules created with your students. If they meet the three E's, then they are good rules.

Figure 2.2   Three E's of Rule Setting

❑ *Essential.* Are they really important? Do they encompass a number of situations?

❑ *Enforceable.* Am I able to follow through with these rules? (Remember, students focus on whether you are fair and apply the same rules to everyone. If you don't think you can consistently apply the rule, don't post the rule.)

❑ *Effective.* Do these rules make sense? Do the routines work? (Sometimes even the best-planned routines fall flat.)

Less Is More

Instead of trying to develop rules that anticipate any possible misbehavior imaginable, create a few general rules that guide students toward acceptable behavior regardless of the specific issue or context. It is also a good idea to phrase rules in a positive way. Avoid using words such as *don't* or *refrain from* in your rules. Rather, express your rules in terms of desirable behavior—the behavior you'd like to see in your classroom. Instead of using the rule "Don't interrupt others," tell students what you would like them to do to avoid interrupting others, such as "Raise your hand when you wish to speak" or "Use appropriate voice levels when you talk." Table 2.2 shows how you might align your rules with your classroom goals.

Common Terms for Classroom Rules

➤ Class Agreements
➤ Classroom Constitution
➤ Class Norms
➤ Class Standards
➤ Class Expectations
➤ Class Rules

Formalizing and Posting Rules

As you develop your list of rules, keep in mind that the language you use should reflect the climate and attitudes you wish to foster within your classroom. The mere term *rules* conjures up a rather undemocratic climate, whereas the terms *agreements* and *expectations* convey a different feeling altogether. Be sure to use terms that are consistent with any established terms used in your school, department, or grade level. (See the box "Common Terms for Classroom Rules.")

Table 2.2   Aligning Classroom Rules With Classroom Goals

Goal	What Does It Look Like?	Sample Rules and Procedures
Establish and protect a productive and organized learning environment.	• Students come to class ready to learn and prepared with materials. • Students are actively engaged in learning activities with minimal downtime. • Transitions are planned and smoothly implemented with minimal confusion and loss of time. • Students follow procedures to get their needs met without interrupting the rest of the class. • The school and class are committed to reducing or eliminating interruptions during instructional time.	• Come to class ready to learn. • Engage appropriately in the class activities. • Raise your hand if you have something to contribute. • Move to the next activity quickly and quietly. • Respond quickly to teacher's directions and signals. • Respect your fellow learner through your actions. • Act in a way that doesn't interrupt the others' learning.
Provide an environment that fosters respect, independence, safety, and acceptance of all students.	• Students' abilities increase so they can do more tasks with less assistance by the end of the year. • Students understand the rules, routines, and procedures that communicate the teacher's expectations for their learning and behavior. • Students work collaboratively, using respectful communication and actions. • Students demonstrate respect for different opinions, backgrounds, and abilities.	• Be safe. • Be responsible for your own learning and be considerate of the learning of others. • Act respectfully toward everyone in this classroom, even if you disagree with their ideas or find theirs to be different from yours. • Support each other in group learning.
Ensure that all students meet the learning standards.	• Activities are linked to specific learning goals. • Lessons are organized around the standards. • The learning environment is set up to accommodate all types of learners. • Instructional strategies reflect a variety of techniques in order to reach all students.	• Be an active participant. • Complete your work on time and with your best effort.

Whatever you call your rules—agreements, norms, standards, or another term—you must state them in terms that students understand. Consider using "I" statements, such as "I will come to class ready to learn." (For more information on "I" statements, see the box on page 31 titled "'I' Statements.") Make sure that students have seen or heard examples of the desired behaviors and contrasting undesired behaviors. Review these behaviors routinely, reinforcing and reminding students of them and their importance. List and display your class rules where all students can view them; the list will serve as an ongoing reminder of your expectations. You may choose to include the three major goals presented earlier in this chapter (Figure 2.1), listing the rules under each goal. This helps students connect their behavior to their learning. If you teach older students (Grade 4 and above), you may wish to ask students to sign agreements that show their understanding and acceptance of the rules. Some teachers also ask parents to show their support for classroom rules by signing a copy.

> ## "I" Statements
>
> When students are encouraged to use "I" statements, they tend to take ownership of their behavior and feelings (Nelson, Lott, & Glenn, 2000). Challenge students to use "I" statements when they are engaged in conflicts, experiencing frustration, or discussing behavioral expectations (such as classroom rules). For example, help a student rephrase a blaming statement such as "Stephen made me mad because he teased me!" into an "I" statement by asking the student to fill in the blank: "When Stephen teased me, I felt _____." Using "I" statements is a powerful strategy to help students identify and take responsibility for their own actions.

The Other Part of the Formula: Procedures

Even when you have developed the most thoughtful rules possible to guide classroom behavior, if you don't set procedures for common classroom routines, you may still end up with chaos. Procedures are the critical organizers that help your instruction take place. Your goal is to determine the processes necessary to maximize learning time and minimize wasted time. Be sure to develop and teach procedures for all routine actions that occur within your classroom.

To get started, take an imaginary walk through a typical school day. List all the things students must do from the time they enter your classroom until the time they leave it at the end of the school day. Then go one step further and think about an atypical day. What special circumstances or events need special procedures to avoid chaos and minimize disruption in student learning? Create clear and effective management strategies to handle fire drills, assemblies, sick students, lab experiments, and other infrequent happenings in your classroom.

As a starting point, you should identify clear procedures for the following activities:

- Entrance and exit from the classroom
- Transitions between activities and classrooms
- Assemblies
- Recess
- Fire drills
- Bathroom breaks and passes (See the box on page 32 titled "Managing the Restroom.")
- Line-up procedures
- Student-teacher appointments
- Attendance
- Lunch count
- Homework routines (distributing and collecting assignments)
- Free time

- Forgotten or incomplete work
- Makeup work (due to absence)
- Materials (retrieving and caring for them)
- Library visits, including checking out books

Regardless of your students' age, do not expect procedures to fall naturally into place or assume that students know what to do in every situation. Students must specifically hear your expectations and know your systems for classroom management. The time you take to establish procedures and routines is well worth the investment and will help support your goal of an uninterrupted learning experience.

Transitions: Getting From A to Z Without Stopping at J

Teachers commonly forget to set procedures for connections or transitions between activities. However, the way students move from one activity to the next can make or break those activities. Remember, the goal is to maximize learning time. Use the four P's—Plan, Prepare, Practice, and Praise—to ensure smooth transitions (see Figure 2.3).

Managing the Restroom

Create two passes—one for the girls' restroom and one for the boys' restroom. Place the passes in a holder on the wall or near the bulletin board closest to the door. Explain the procedure clearly: "When you need to use the restroom, ask permission from the teacher, excuse yourself, and take a restroom pass with you." Talk to students about appropriate times to go to the restroom. Explain that it is not appropriate to leave in the middle of the lesson. However, be sure students understand if they really need to use the restroom, they are allowed to leave anytime throughout the day. (You don't want to have to clean up an accident after assuming incorrectly that a student was faking.)

Figure 2.3   The Four P's for Successful Transitions

Use these steps during your first few weeks to establish classroom procedures:

- ❑ *Plan* the steps in the transition. Be proactive and realistic about the steps in any transition. Ask yourself questions such as, do students have materials to put away? Break tasks into small steps.
- ❑ *Prepare* your students for each transition. First, eliminate the element of surprise by writing your agenda on the board or by cueing students. Make sure students clearly understand, before they start moving, what it is they are supposed to do next. Second, know which students (e.g., those with attention difficulties or autism) might have difficulty with transitions. Rapid shifts without adequate preparation may upset or disorient these students. Third, make sure students know the procedures for turning in homework or parent notes. This will eliminate interruptions when you are trying to start class.
- ❑ *Practice* moving from activity to activity with students. Use signals to gain students' attention and to cue them for the transition.
- ❑ *Praise* students for making effective transitions. Set class or individual goals related to transitions and celebrate their attainment.

Sponge Activities

You may find yourself with a little extra time in the classroom, or you may find that a number of students have already completed their work and need something to keep them from distracting others. You can use sponge activities to overcome this dilemma. Sponge activities are short tasks that quickly focus or engage your students. These tasks may reinforce general problem solving or specific skills that students are currently learning, or they may merely supplement the curriculum. Sponge activities are not only effective during transitions; they are also great energizers for times when students' attention and interest are dwindling.

Use sponge activities to transform lost time into valuable learning time. Some teachers use sponge activities as students enter the room to ensure that students become focused and ready for learning. These teachers post the task on the board or leave clear instructions on every student desk.

Figure 2.4 shows some ideas for sponge activities. For more ideas, see the Worthwhile Web Sites box.

> Sponge activities are short tasks that quickly focus or engage your students. These tasks may reinforce general problem solving or specific skills that students are currently learning, or they may merely supplement the curriculum.

Figure 2.4   Ideas for Sponge Activities

- ❑ Write as many words as you can think of that are derived from the root word *life*.
- ❑ Write the names of the states in alphabetical order.
- ❑ List words that rhyme with *hay*.
- ❑ List pairs of rhyming words.
- ❑ List all the ways we use math in our lives.
- ❑ Write sentences in which every word begins with the same letter.
- ❑ Use each letter in your name to create a word that describes you.
- ❑ List pairs of opposite words.
- ❑ Use vocabulary words to write a paragraph.
- ❑ Use as many words as possible to describe the object at the front of the class.
- ❑ List all the countries you can remember.
- ❑ Calculate the number of fingers and toes in our class.
- ❑ Create a story about the picture shown on the overhead.

Worthwhile Web Sites

The following Web sites feature sponge activities:

A to Z Teacher Stuff
(atozteacherstuff.com/tips/Sponge_and_Transition_Activities)

Teachnet.com (www.teachnet.com/powertools/take5)

Delegation: Empowering Students Through Class Jobs

In addition to setting classroom rules and procedures, teachers can manage their classrooms by assigning students to perform classroom jobs. Although it seems obvious to involve students in simple classroom jobs, many teachers forget to do so. Assigning class jobs to students not only minimizes the number of tasks you must do; it also actively engages your students and instills a sense of responsibility within them. Class jobs even enhance student learning. Students who file graded papers practice their alphabetizing skills and learn overall strategies for organizing information. You may also design jobs to help students gain competence in areas that are difficult for them (such as delivering messages to the office). For certain jobs, you may enlist teams of students rather than individuals.

If you are unsure about which tasks you should delegate to your students, ask them. Even young children can help identify jobs in your classroom. Be sure to check on your school's policies regarding student liability for moving equipment or using certain machines, such as paper cutters. Always make sure that you or another qualified adult appropriately supervises students at all times. Figure 2.5 offers some examples of classroom jobs.

> **Teachers can manage their classrooms by assigning students to perform classroom jobs.**

Figure 2.5   Classroom Jobs

- ❑ Organizing and straightening materials
- ❑ Writing class newsletters
- ❑ Grading papers
- ❑ Collating papers
- ❑ Sharpening pencils
- ❑ Cleaning white boards and chalkboards
- ❑ Tending plants and animals in the room
- ❑ Taking attendance or lunch counts
- ❑ Returning graded papers
- ❑ Gathering information for absent students

■ KEEPING BEHAVIORS IN CHECK

Not surprisingly, even after you have established your class rules and procedures, a small percentage of students will still break them. Before this happens, make a plan for dealing with misbehavior. The best approach is to establish positive consequences (rewards) and negative consequences (punishments) for your major categories of rules.

When you are developing positive and negative consequences, be sure to reference your classroom management goals (such as those in Figure 2.1). Consequences should help preserve instructional time and serve to develop students' social skills and interactions. Consider using class meetings or other group processes to determine consequences. When students determine and agree on the consequences, they are likely to accept them more readily. (Note: If you allow students to help develop consequences, be sure to play an active role and ensure the appropriateness of the consequences.)

Low-key teacher responses can also help keep behaviors in check. These include walking around the classroom and staying close to certain students, saying the student's name at any given time, and redirecting negative behavior before it becomes a full-blown discipline issue.

Positive Consequences

Research has shown that the best way to encourage desirable behavior is to reward or reinforce it when it happens (Kazdin, 1973; Madsen, Becker, & Thomas, 1968). A positive reinforcement (a consequence that promotes a desired behavior) can be as simple as a smile or a high five or as complex as a point system. No matter what approach you choose, rewarding or reinforcing the things you want your students to do increases the likelihood that they'll do them again. Positive reinforcement systems can be used with individuals or groups.

> **Rewarding or reinforcing the things you want your students to do increases the likelihood that they'll do them again.**

Individual Management Strategies

Typical individual reinforcement strategies include compliments, fuzzy-grams, Caught in the Act, and class stores or banks.

Compliments. Used appropriately, compliments accomplish a number of goals. First, compliments serve as a direct and sincere way to tell students when they do something you appreciate. Second, compliments model appropriate social skills. Third, compliments provide an opportunity to connect with the student on a personal level.

The key is to make sure that the compliment is specific to the behavior. In addition, compliments should be phrased and delivered in such a way that they are age appropriate for the students. A well-intended compliment to an adolescent can have the opposite effect if it seems mushy to the student's peers. Here are some examples of compliments that are specific and avoid mushiness:

- I really appreciate the way that Table B has cleaned up so quickly.
- I can tell that you really put a lot of work into the organization of this paper. I can really see your effort.
- Thank you for all your help today. It's been a busy day, and the way that you've gotten right to work has helped us all.

Fuzzy-Grams. Students love to receive notes, especially from their teachers. Notes are especially effective with students who are sensitive about being singled out by your attention in class. Set up a rotating system to ensure that every student receives a note periodically. It's easy to skip over students who are quiet or don't stand out. Some teachers use a monthly checklist of students' names to ensure each student receives attention. Look for something positive in each student and write a quick note. You may write about how much you appreciate a student's hard work on a particular day or how his or her input made a difference in a class discussion.

Consider using these additional types of positive communication:

- Notes home
- Phone calls home
- Notes to or from the principal
- Notes from an older student
- E-mail messages

Caught in the Act. In this strategy, students are randomly awarded tickets when they demonstrate desired behaviors. You may choose to highlight a specific behavior (e.g., raising hands) or reinforce a number of behaviors (e.g., answering questions correctly, being courteous to fellow students, or completing homework). When you award a ticket, be sure the student knows what he or she did to earn it. Ask the student to write his or her name on the ticket and deposit it in a large jar. Draw three to five winning tickets from the jar on a daily or weekly basis. (Students or the teacher may draw the tickets.) Reward the winners in some fashion, such as giving them a special treat, dismissing them early, or allowing them to do another appropriate activity. This strategy is easily adapted to any grade level by merely changing the rewards.

Class Stores or Banks. You may adapt Caught in the Act by allowing winning ticket holders to exchange their tickets for special prizes on a weekly or monthly basis, similar to exchanging tickets for prizes at arcades. Prizes might include colorful pencils and markers, unusual erasers, book covers, get-out-of-homework passes, and afterschool time with the teacher, among others.

You may also adapt the strategy to create a class "bank." This system incorporates practice of math application skills (e.g., adding deposits, subtracting withdrawals, balancing a checkbook, and budgeting). It also allows students opportunities to serve in assigned roles (e.g., bank teller, accountant, manager) on a rotating basis.

Class stores and class banks are powerful reinforcement strategies. However, be aware that they are time consuming and require significant time to organize. Classroom volunteers and parent donations can help the process.

Neutral Strategies for Getting Individual Students Back on Task

Now and then, students may stray from the task and may distract others in the process. Most of the time, these occasional off-task behaviors can be handled with some quick and neutral strategies that don't distract from your instruction. These responses include physical proximity (staying close to students) and verbal cues to prompt students to reengage in appropriate behavior. By not saying anything but simply moving closer to a student who is off task, you're prompting that student to pay attention. You can also redirect students' attention by asking questions or merely saying their name ("I see John knows what to do right now" or "Oh I hope Table 3 can make good decisions right now").

Some students may seek ways to entertain themselves with something other than the assigned task, especially if the task is a difficult one. By keeping tabs on the students who might be easily frustrated (or even bored), you can get a sense of when they begin to stray and find a way to direct their attention back to the activity. You might also come up with an activity designed to give them a break from the frustration (this gives them permission to go off task for a bit, then come back to it with a fresh outlook).

The Power of Many: Group Management Strategies

There is much to be said about the power of groups, whether the whole class or smaller teams. Call it peer pressure, group accountability, or a sense of community: Most students are naturally compelled to work as part of a team. Teachers can use this fact to their advantage by employing group management strategies frequently to ensure a smoothly running classroom.

> **Most students are naturally compelled to work as part of a team.**

First, divide your class into groups by using table groups, rows, lab teams, cooperative learning groups, or some other logical system. Second, foster student leadership by assigning team captains on a rotating basis. Third, be sure that team members clearly understand their responsibilities and your expectations. Fourth, encourage the groups to compete in a friendly way and on the basis of their performance of the target behaviors. Common group reinforcement strategies include marbles in the jar, lunch bunch club, and preferred seating.

Marbles in the Jar. In this strategy, each team has a jar, located in a visible spot. When teams display target behaviors (e.g., participating actively, completing work, answering questions correctly), add marbles (or beans) to their jar. The team that fills its jar (or reaches a preset line) first receives a reward. You may adapt this activity by counting the marbles at the end of the week and rewarding the team that has the most marbles.

Lunch Bunch Club. In this strategy, teams with the most appropriate classroom behavior, or highest number of points, are allowed to eat lunch with the teacher. Ask the winning team to bring their lunches and gather together with you. As an alternative, you may purchase lunch for the group using funds from the parent-teacher association. Be sure to inform the principal and the students' parents in advance that you are allowing students to attend a lunch bunch.

Preferred Seating. In this variation, teams that earn the most points choose their seat locations for the next period (e.g., a week, a month, or a quarter). Before using this option, be sure that you have considered the needs of other students in your class. For example, students with hearing or visual impairments should receive preferential seating. In addition, students with attention deficits benefit from placement closer to the front of the room.

Negative Consequences

Somehow, sometime, someone will break a classroom rule. Many teachers have difficulty dealing with this aspect of classroom management. On one hand, teachers want to ensure the learning of all students, and on the other, teachers want to be liked. The key is to be prepared. It's quite common to be so surprised by a student's misbehavior that you respond with inappropriate consequences or in a way that makes the situation worse. While it's not easy to anticipate the problems you might have or predict students' motivations, you can review your classroom rules and guess what behaviors students might demonstrate if they don't follow the rules. Once you have identified the possibilities, you can decide on your consequences in advance. Do not rely on ad-libbing your consequences. Ad-libbing will only lead to inconsistency and a tendency to provide inappropriately harsh punishments.

> **Do not rely on ad-libbing your consequences.**

Find out whether your school or department uses a hierarchy of responses or has some other specific plan for dealing with problematic behavior. If there is no established system, you can choose from a variety of systems of consequences for your students who violate the rules. Consider your students' age, past experiences (e.g., was this system used by their previous teacher?), and the amount of time and effort it will take you to apply the system consistently. Use the guidelines shown in Figure 2.6 to determine appropriate consequences.

Figure 2.6   Guidelines for Determining Appropriate Consequences

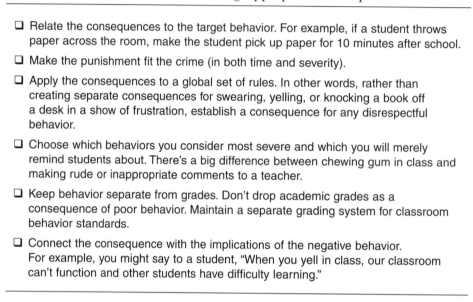

❑ Relate the consequences to the target behavior. For example, if a student throws paper across the room, make the student pick up paper for 10 minutes after school.

❑ Make the punishment fit the crime (in both time and severity).

❑ Apply the consequences to a global set of rules. In other words, rather than creating separate consequences for swearing, yelling, or knocking a book off a desk in a show of frustration, establish a consequence for any disrespectful behavior.

❑ Choose which behaviors you consider most severe and which you will merely remind students about. There's a big difference between chewing gum in class and making rude or inappropriate comments to a teacher.

❑ Keep behavior separate from grades. Don't drop academic grades as a consequence of poor behavior. Maintain a separate grading system for classroom behavior standards.

❑ Connect the consequence with the implications of the negative behavior. For example, you might say to a student, "When you yell in class, our classroom can't function and other students have difficulty learning."

As a new teacher, you are establishing your own teaching style. The manner in which you follow through on students' positive and negative behaviors signals to your students whether you are a pushover teacher, an extremely controlling teacher, or a teacher with high expectations for student learning. Without question, you must avoid becoming a pushover or a controlling teacher. Veteran teachers agree that the most effective approach is to be firm but calm. A matter-of-fact attitude helps you remain neutral rather than taking personal offense and possibly overreacting to a student's misbehavior. If you balance a matter-of-fact style with warm, respectful, and personal connections with your students, they will understand and respect the rules, and they will more readily accept consequences for their behavior.

> **Veteran teachers agree that the most effective approach is to be firm but calm.**

Two teachers can apply the same consequence but receive different responses because they deliver the consequence in different ways. If a teacher angrily confronts a student in front of the student's peers, the teacher probably will not get the desired response: a positive change in the student's behavior. However, if the teacher speaks privately and frankly to the student about a concern, the student will likely respond in a more positive manner. Remember, your goal is to elicit a positive change in students' behavior, so your approach is important. Consider the guidelines shown in Figure 2.7.

Figure 2.7   Effective Consequences for Negative Behavior

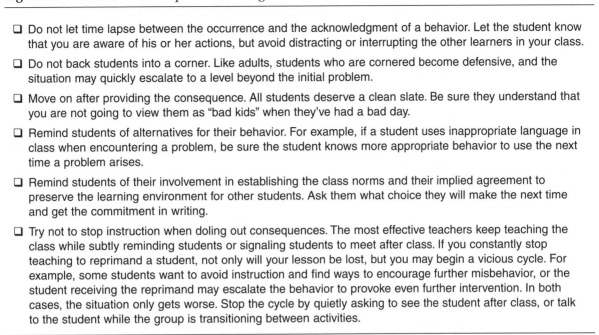

- ❑ Do not let time lapse between the occurrence and the acknowledgment of a behavior. Let the student know that you are aware of his or her actions, but avoid distracting or interrupting the other learners in your class.

- ❑ Do not back students into a corner. Like adults, students who are cornered become defensive, and the situation may quickly escalate to a level beyond the initial problem.

- ❑ Move on after providing the consequence. All students deserve a clean slate. Be sure they understand that you are not going to view them as "bad kids" when they've had a bad day.

- ❑ Remind students of alternatives for their behavior. For example, if a student uses inappropriate language in class when encountering a problem, be sure the student knows more appropriate behavior to use the next time a problem arises.

- ❑ Remind students of their involvement in establishing the class norms and their implied agreement to preserve the learning environment for other students. Ask them what choice they will make the next time and get the commitment in writing.

- ❑ Try not to stop instruction when doling out consequences. The most effective teachers keep teaching the class while subtly reminding students or signaling students to meet after class. If you constantly stop teaching to reprimand a student, not only will your lesson be lost, but you may begin a vicious cycle. For example, some students want to avoid instruction and find ways to encourage further misbehavior, or the student receiving the reprimand may escalate the behavior to provoke even further intervention. In both cases, the situation only gets worse. Stop the cycle by quietly asking to see the student after class, or talk to the student while the group is transitioning between activities.

Catching Behaviors Before They Escalate

It is much easier to prevent the escalation of behavior than to deal with it after it has happened. By anticipating the actions that feed into negative behaviors, you can deter potential causes and prevent the escalation of misbehavior. Every behavior is triggered and sustained by outside stimuli. For example, check the environmental conditions. Has the classroom gotten too noisy? Is the classroom activity level too stimulating? Look at the task or activity. Have students been on a task too long? Are some students bored? Are some students unable to complete the assigned task?

You can prevent the escalation of misbehavior through individual and group strategies. The following paragraphs describe these strategies.

Individual Strategy: Self-Monitoring

This strategy fosters independence and reduces the need for ongoing feedback. Foster self-monitoring by asking students to evaluate themselves on their work habits, interactions, and engagement in the learning activity. At certain points during class time, ask students to stop and self-monitor. Tell students to rate themselves from 1 to 5, showing their rating with their fingers. Post a rating scale or rubric for behaviors (e.g., 5 = I'm definitely getting this stuff and following the rules, 4 = I'm doing pretty well but could focus a little more, 3 = I am having a little trouble, 2 = Help! and 1 = I'm way off base!). Self-monitoring allows you to quickly survey your students' engagement with an activity.

Group Strategies

Names on the Board. Write students' names on the blackboard when they break a rule. Add checks for repeat offenses. Determine consequences for each level. For example, the student's name on the board means 5 minutes of lost recess, one check means the student will be benched during recess, and two checks means you will make a phone call home.

Pulling Cards. Create a chart with a pocket for each student. Place four cards (green, yellow, blue, and red) within each pocket. Students each start on green. If they break a class rule, they move to yellow (caution) and receive a warning. If they make a second infraction, they move to blue and receive a consequence (e.g., benching at recess or losing free time). If they make a third infraction, they move to red and receive a note to their parents. This strategy works well with younger children.

In the Zone. Designate one magnet or clothespin per student. Determine zone names to describe whether students are following rules or struggling. You may have zones called Wow!, Good!, Uh-Oh!, and Oh No! Start each student's clothespin at Wow! and move it to a different zone as warranted by their behavior. You may assign point values to each zone. For example, students in the Wow! zone receive four points for the day; students in Good! receive three points; and so on. You may also assign negative consequences for students who end up in the Uh-Oh! or Oh No! zones.

◾ DEALING WITH SEVERE BEHAVIOR

When confronted with severe behavior, consider the suggestions already mentioned in this chapter as well as the guidelines shown in Figure 2.8. Following these guidelines will help you de-escalate rather than escalate problem behaviors and also will allow you to approach difficult situations with professionalism and good judgment. You may also choose to set up individual contracts and behavior management plans to handle severe behavioral challenges.

Behavior Management Plans and Individual Contracts

For a variety of reasons, some students need more individualized assistance if they are to demonstrate appropriate behavior in the classroom. To work effectively with these students, you may be required to develop a behavior management plan or individual behavior contract.

Behavior Management Plans

Before developing a behavior management plan, take time to analyze the student's behavior. The following questions can help you gain insight into the student's behavior and identify some solutions for helping the student make more appropriate behavioral choices:

- *What are the triggers of this behavior? When does it occur?* Does it happen during a certain time of day or during a particular activity? Are other students involved?

Figure 2.8   Survival Tips for Dealing With Severe Behavior

To decrease the escalation of misbehavior, avoid these Don'ts and apply the Do's:

Don'ts

❑ Don't take the misbehavior personally.

❑ Don't yell.

❑ Don't touch a student.

❑ Don't argue.

❑ Don't cry.

❑ Don't bully.

❑ Don't admonish or embarrass the student in front of other students.

❑ Don't accuse. Ask questions first.

❑ Don't threaten with a consequence you cannot follow through with or should not use.

Do's

❑ Anticipate situations that might result in negative behavior (e.g., overstimulating activities, pending consequences)

❑ Remind the student of the rule in a matter-of-fact manner. Ask to speak to the student privately.

❑ Use your existing supports (e.g., psychologist, administrators, support teachers, teaching peers) at the school.

❑ Follow through with consequences.

❑ Depersonalize your thinking.

❑ Set the problem aside until you or the student calms down.

❑ Use strategies to redirect students who easily escalate into inappropriate activities. For example, if a student begins to look agitated or bored, engage the student in an activity that he or she will likely enjoy (e.g., helping pass out papers). Check with the student about how he or she is feeling.

❑ Use "I" statements.

❑ Acknowledge the student's frustration.

❑ Communicate with your administrator and the student's parents.

❑ Document major incidents. Write down the date(s) of the occurrence(s), a detailed account of the incident(s), your responses, and the follow-up(s).

- *What is the function or purpose of the behavior? What is the student trying to achieve through the behavior?* Does the student wish to avoid an activity? Is the student seeking attention? Is the student trying to engage other students?

- *What seems to make a difference in the student's behavior?* When do you observe the undesired behavior the least? Will the student respond to a certain type of structure or prompt?

Answering these questions empowers you to develop an effective management plan. Ideally, you will not be doing this by yourself but will solicit involvement from the student, a parent, or an outside observer such as your school administrator or other professional. Together, you can create a plan that contains the following elements:

- *The target behavior that you want to increase.* Suppose a student continually leaves his or her seat and walks around the room. You would want to increase the time the student stays seated. Also include the acceptable level that you'd like to see occur. You may decide to focus on the behavior only during certain subjects or times of the day.

- *The plan for anticipating and interrupting the triggers that result in undesirable behavior and the plan for positively reinforcing the desired behavior after it occurs.* Perhaps you see the student getting antsy, and you anticipate that he will begin to wander. You may walk over to the student and provide praise for staying in his seat even when he's feeling antsy.

- *The plan for monitoring the changes in behavior and communicating progress with the parents and student.* For example, keep a clipboard handy; look up every 15 minutes during your 1-hour lesson and make a simple check mark if the student is staying seated.

Individual Contracts

One of your goals as a teacher is to foster student independence. An individual contract supports this goal by placing the responsibility for appropriate behavior on the student and requiring the student to make a commitment to change. Not only do individual contracts bring about positive change in the targeted behaviors, but because they are created and monitored by the teacher and the student together, they also strengthen the rapport between teacher and student. Follow the steps shown in Figure 2.9 as you work with the student to develop an individual contract.

Severe Behavior: Getting Assistance

From time to time, one or two students may offer particular challenges in classroom behavior. If you encounter these students in your classroom, it does not mean that you're a bad teacher. It simply means that you must employ different strategies. Use these resources when working with students with challenging behavior:

- *Seek out existing information about the student.* Look in the student's cumulative folder for comments or information regarding past behavioral concerns. You may find that the student has a history of similar behaviors, and the file may offer effective interventions or strategies for handling these behaviors.

Figure 2.9   Steps for Developing Individual Contracts

1. Identify and agree on the behavior to be changed. Describe where and when the behavior most frequently occurs. (For example, "On the playground, I will take turns appropriately during handball.")

2. Establish realistic goals for changing the behavior. ("I will do this for five days in a row.")

3. Identify how long the behavior plan will be in effect. ("We will check my progress on December 1.")

4. Identify reinforcements and consequences. ("If I meet my goal, I will get to eat lunch with my teacher.")

5. Self-evaluate the success of the program each day using a chart or check-in procedure.

- *Get in touch with the student's parents.* Anytime you have a student in your class who offers challenging behaviors, talk to the student's parents. Not only is it good practice to inform parents when their child is having difficulties; it also gives you helpful insights into the student. The parents may be able to help you design a plan to help the student with the behavior. Assure the parents that you are interested in helping their child succeed in the classroom and that you would like to work with them as a team. Be clear that you are not judging their parenting skills and that you do not have a personal grudge against their child.

- *Talk to your fellow teachers.* Experienced teachers can provide great insights in dealing with students with challenging behaviors. Never feel embarrassed about seeking assistance. Nobody knows it all, especially during the first years of teaching. Tapping the experience of veteran teachers saves you time and provides many good, classroom-tested ideas. If you have access to the student's previous teachers, ask them to explain which strategies were successful with the student.

- *Call in the student study or intervention team.* Every public school is required to have a team of educators who meet on a regular basis to discuss students who have difficulty learning. This group is typically called a student study team or a student intervention team and is charged with providing regular interventions. If you have a student who has significant needs due to his or her behavior, you can make a referral to the team. The school will have a referral process. You will be asked to participate as a member of the team, provide background information about the student, describe your concerns about the student, explain the impact of the student's behavior on his or her learning, discuss strategies you have used, and provide data on the results of the strategies. The team will discuss possible ideas for improving the student's behavior in the classroom. The team may recommend additional meetings with the student's parents, or the team may refer you to other resources for support.

- *Speak to the school social worker or psychologist.* Many schools employ full- or part-time professionals who are specially trained to assist students having difficulty in school. These professionals are there to support you. Set aside time to speak with one of them and, if possible, ask him or her to observe in the classroom. Find out whether your school has policies that require you to obtain the parents' permission before asking the social worker or psychologist to do an observation.

■ ESTABLISHING A SENSE OF COMMUNITY

One of your major classroom management goals is to provide an environment that fosters respect, independence, safety, and acceptance of all students. A sense of community in the classroom helps you achieve this goal. You can establish a sense of community through class meetings, traditions, celebrations, greetings, and character education.

Active Learning Strategies

Using active learning strategies in your classroom will not only assist your class management but also increase the likelihood that all students will be engaged in learning. Here are some strategies:

➤ *Think-Pair-Share.* In this strategy, students are asked to first think about an idea, pair with a partner to discuss it, and share their ideas with a group.

➤ *One-Liners.* One-liners can be used when you would like to get input from every student quickly. In this strategy, each student (by rows or around a circle) makes a comment or states an idea that is only one sentence in length (in other words, a one-liner).

➤ *Showdown.* Following a question or prompt that requires a brief response, students in a group each write their answer or thoughts on a piece of paper or small whiteboard. When everyone in the group is ready, the leader says "Showdown," and the students each show their answer. Discussion ensues.

Class Meetings

Class meetings offer an opportunity for each class member to focus on relevant issues and contribute equally to solutions. Use meetings to discuss options and responses to the various activities students encounter in the classroom. Hold meetings to establish class policies and routines. Convene forums to make decisions that affect the class, such as plans for upcoming holiday celebrations or ideas for cheering up a student who is in the hospital.

You may either schedule regular class meetings or convene meetings as issues or problems arise. Many teachers schedule weekly or monthly meetings, in which all students are expected to participate. Middle and high schools sometimes offer advisory periods to allow students to participate in class meetings.

Meetings offer students excellent opportunities for practicing effective communication and problem-solving skills. However, merely bringing students together does not result in a positive and productive class meeting. You must facilitate and guide meetings so students learn effective strategies and function as a community within class meetings. These guidelines will help you:

1. Tell students to sit in a circle so that they can see each other. This seating pattern discourages students from sinking into the background and becoming nonparticipants.

2. Use active learning strategies to maximize student participation. See the strategies in the box titled "Active Learning Strategies."

3. Follow a consistent agenda so students can practice in each section. Your agenda may be
   a. Kudos (appreciation and recognition) (5 minutes)
   b. Introduction of the topic; posing the key question (2 minutes)
   c. Responses to the question or topic (e.g., brainstorming, role-playing, think-pair-share) (10 minutes)
   d. Closing or reflection (5 minutes)

Traditions

Creating and maintaining traditions establishes classroom community. Consider using the following traditions in your classroom:

- Special card, pin, crown, or seat for birthday students
- Welcome activities for new students
- Farewell activities for departing students
- End-of-year ceremony
- Parent day (e.g., students cook breakfast)

Celebrations

A learning-centered classroom offers many opportunities for including celebrations. Avoid overdoing holiday celebrations. (In December, many classrooms' entire focus is on winter play.) Instead, consider ways to celebrate learning in your classroom. Give a special cheer or award each time a student achieves a certain level of competency in writing or demonstrates significant improvement in behavior. Recognize and celebrate students who do special things in the class or the community (e.g., random acts of kindness, powerful problem solving). Embed celebrations into units by holding culminating activities such as pioneer days or science nights.

Greetings

Nothing establishes your relationship with students more easily than learning their names and then using their names on a daily basis. Greet students as they enter and leave the room each day. Say something nice about them or wish them a good day. Don't use a greeting as just an opportunity to remind students of their work. Let students know that you are glad to see them. Encourage this type of interaction between students as well.

> **Learn students' names and use them on a daily basis.**

Character Education

Many state and district curricula include character education. Character education is typically infused across the curriculum and

---

Worthwhile Web Sites

These Web sites offer information regarding character education programs and other useful ideas you might like to implement in your classroom:

Character Counts! (www.charactercounts.org)

Character Development Foundation (www.charactered.org)

CharacterEd.net (www.charactered.net)

International Center for Character Education (www.teachvalues.org/icce)

in the daily routine rather than taught as a specific subject or course. Character education seeks to develop students' character traits and encourages students to use these traits in the school and community. Use your school's character education program, or if your school doesn't have such a program, create a program of your own. (See Worthwhile Web Sites for character education resources.)

■ KEEPING THINGS TOGETHER EVEN WHEN YOU'RE NOT THERE: EFFECTIVE SUBSTITUTE PLANS

Now and then, due to illness or the need to attend a special training session or meeting, you use the services of a substitute teacher. The word *substitute* often conjures up a vision of a timid and confused fill-in teacher surrounded by chaos and student saboteurs. The good news is that you can shatter that image and increase the chances that your sub and your students will have a successful experience while you are absent.

> **Make it a practice to leave substitute plans on your desk each day when you leave school.**

Make it a practice to leave substitute plans on your desk each day when you leave school. Many schools require you to keep a set of lesson plans on file in the school office as well. Some teachers e-mail plans to a fellow teacher or to the principal if they were unable to prepare plans prior to leaving school. In addition to creating lesson plans, many teachers develop a three-ring binder at the beginning of the year that includes a wide range of useful information. Follow these tips to create a positive substitute experience:

- *Provide a student seating chart.* Include student names and some notes pertaining to each student. (For example, indicate students who are learning English or need to go to the office at a certain time for medication.)

- *Provide students' pictures and names.* If possible, take a class picture (or individual snapshots of your students) and cut out each student's picture. Place each picture on an index card with the student's name and any specific notes. The substitute can use these cards to randomly call on students during class discussion or to identify students whose behaviors are particularly helpful or unhelpful.

- *Develop a generic lesson plan.* In the event that you are unable to provide specific lesson plans, provide a general framework of the day. Describe common routines and procedures, including the manner in which students are expected to transition from place to place. In addition, list possible sponge activities that the substitute can use to fill time or pull the class together when things seem to be moving in a negative direction.

- *Assign student ambassadors.* Ask students to sign up in advance to assist substitutes with certain aspects of the day. One student may assist the substitute in understanding the process for going to lunch, and another may assist with the process for distributing materials for lab experiments. If you know you will be away on a specific day, be sure, before you leave, to review students' roles for assisting the substitute.

- *Include a map of the school.* Mark key areas, such as the teachers' lounge, restroom, and office.

- *List key people who are available to assist the substitute.* Mention the teacher in an adjoining classroom or the assistant principal involved with your department. Be sure to include room numbers or intercom extensions, if appropriate.

- *Establish a feedback system with the substitute.* Encourage the substitute to communicate the events of the day, any significant incidents, and students who stood out for their helpful (or not-so-helpful) behaviors. Some teachers provide the substitute with a rating sheet for students' cooperation and behavior. These teachers reward individuals, groups, or the whole class for high ratings. For example, if the class gets 4 out of 4 possible points, the teacher may refrain from assigning homework the next day. When students are aware of this system in advance, they tend to rise to the teacher's expectations.

GETTING BACK CONTROL WHEN ALL IS LOST   ■

All teachers, regardless of their level of experience, have bad days. You can approach these days with a few easy strategies. First, admit that you are human. Students will recognize that while your intentions were good, you may not have anticipated an event that ended up throwing your schedule into a tizzy. Second, take a breath and get centered. Ask yourself, What will help my students pull it together? Is this a good time to bring out a sponge activity? Should I get everyone's attention and re-center them with a review of the objectives or an example of what was supposed to happen during the lesson? Third, do not blame the students. Instead, let them know that things didn't work out as you had planned and that you'd like to adjust things. You can even generate feedback and ideas from the students for improving the situation or preventing a similar situation the next time.

STARTER SURVIVOR TIPS   ■

As you have read in this chapter, becoming an effective manager of your classroom is a somewhat complex process that goes beyond rules and procedures. It requires a continuous balance of positive and proactive efforts and will be influenced by your own style, your teaching situation, and your students' needs. Throughout your years of teaching, you will develop your own special techniques that give you this balance and result in a smoothly running classroom. However, as you start this journey, keep the following ideas in mind:

Time Spent Up Front Is a Good Investment

Many effective teachers spend 2 weeks or even longer practicing procedures and transitions with their students. In some schools, students are guided through all the various environments to make sure they know the schoolwide expectations for behavior. Students may be shown appropriate lunchroom behaviors, such as moving through the line, getting rid of trash, and so on. Even if your school doesn't employ this practice, it is something you may want to consider for your own classroom. Doing all this practice may be a bit time consuming but will probably save you from spending a lot of time correcting student behaviors in the future.

Use Your Signals

Have you ever been in a classroom where the teacher is trying to get everyone's attention but is failing miserably? Don't put yourself in that situation. Give your students a signal that cues them that you need their immediate attention. Some teachers use the freeze or statue approach, in which all students are asked to freeze their mouths and bodies. Other teachers ring a bell, use a clicker, or flick the lights. Whatever signal you choose, make sure your students will notice it but that it will not distract students in other classrooms. Train your students from the beginning of the year to respond quickly to this signal. Use it frequently to keep students in practice, and reinforce quick responses to the signal.

> Give your students a signal that cues them that you need their immediate attention.

Have a Backup Plan

Imagine starting class and a student has a seizure. What will you do? Even the most organized teachers can be thrown into a situation that is beyond their control. No matter the situation, stay cool and think on your feet. To give yourself something to fall back on rather than falling apart, establish a backup plan and keep it in mind for such emergencies. Devise the plan by thinking of a worst-case scenario and imagining how to work your way out of it. Check for existing school policies and procedures that may help you. Include your classroom neighbors (teachers across the hall or next door) in your backup plan, especially if you need to leave the classroom in an emergency. Your backup plan should always include a contact to the office via intercom or phone.

> Establish a backup plan and keep it in mind for emergencies.

Rethink and Revise When Necessary

Good instruction and effective procedures should prevent most classroom management problems. However, if you sense that you are spending too much time giving out consequences for rule breaking, ask yourself the following questions:

- What are the behaviors I'm seeing most frequently?
- Have my expectations changed?
- What might be triggering the increased frequency? What is lacking in content, delivery, or management that would fill the gap?
- Can I implement a procedure that would help change this pattern?

A LAST LOOK AT THE TEACHER AS A MANAGER OF THE CLASSROOM ■

As a teacher, you will experience a lot of good days sprinkled with a few not-so-good days. Do your best to keep things in perspective. It's certainly not the end of the world if things don't always go right. In fact, some teachers keep journals of the funny things that happen to them while teaching. There are even contests for teachers to tell stories about their experiences.

RECOMMENDED READINGS ■

Cummings, C. (2000). *Winning strategies for classroom management.* Alexandria, VA: Association for Supervision and Curriculum Development.

Williamson, B. (1998). *A first-year teacher's guidebook: An educational recipe book for success.* Sacramento, CA: Dynamic Teaching Company.

Questions for Reflection

In what areas of classroom management do I feel particularly strong?

_____

_____

_____

_____

_____

_____

What areas do I find challenging?

_____

_____

_____

_____

_____

What is one thing I can do tomorrow to enhance my management system so that learning remains the focus in class?

_____

_____

_____

_____

_____

_____

Teacher as a Designer of Instruction

"WHAT DO MY STUDENTS NEED TO LEARN?"

One of the most overwhelming aspects of teaching is the struggle to determine what your instructional focus—your curriculum—should be. If you are an elementary teacher, you must coordinate multiple subjects and integrate them across an entire school day. If you are a secondary teacher, you may focus on only one or two courses, but the content of those courses may be complex.

Regardless of the level you teach, you must approach the development of your curriculum just as a contractor builds a home: You must examine your blueprint, determine a logical sequence or work plan, assemble your tools, implement the plan, and finally, check that your work passes inspection. This chapter will assist you in identifying your blueprint (standards and concepts), creating your work plan (mapping your year's content), assembling your tools (designing your units), and sequencing and planning your instruction (writing lesson plans). You will find guidelines for each step, from the "what" (content) of your teaching to the "how" (instructional lesson design) of your daily lessons.

■ BEFORE GETTING STARTED

Before you set out your blueprint, consider the four key points shown in Figure 3.1. Each point is discussed in the following paragraphs.

Figure 3.1   Key Points for Planning

- ☛ Teach the adopted curriculum.
- ☛ Don't rely on textbooks alone. (The textbook is not the curriculum.)
- ☛ Build on the existing curriculum.
- ☛ Align activities to standards (what students should know and be able to do).

Teach the Adopted Curriculum

It is your responsibility to teach the adopted state and district curriculum. You are allowed a certain freedom to creatively implement your curriculum. However, you must remember that your teaching must be tied to the adopted curriculum. Virtually all states and districts throughout the United States have adopted standards and curriculum frameworks to guide teachers in their instruction. This approach ensures that all students receive the full education to which they are entitled.

> **Your teaching must be tied to the adopted curriculum.**

Don't Rely on Textbooks Alone

Many teachers approach their curriculum by merely opening their textbooks and following the sequence provided. While textbooks can be effective tools in delivering instruction, you must use them wisely. Textbook publishers design their texts to address the standards and needs of many states. Because publishers sell to a broad market, their books frequently contain information that is irrelevant to your state or district standards. In their efforts to please everyone in every state, publishers produce textbooks that provide broad information without sufficient depth. In addition, the textbooks may omit information that your students need to know. Don't rely on the textbook alone. Instead, use your knowledge of the standards to determine how the text can be used as a tool to support your teaching.

Don't rely on the textbook alone.

Build on the Existing Curriculum

If you are so fortunate as to work in a school that has already established a clear curriculum and has mapped out units based on the standards, use the curriculum and the units. However, you must understand that some teachers use the same units and lessons year after year out of a sense of tradition rather than out of a desire to address the standards adequately. Therefore, carefully examine existing documents and traditional practices to ensure that they are appropriate and meet curriculum standards.

Align Activities to Standards

Your goal is to ensure that students gain the knowledge and skills targeted by the curriculum. Student achievement of the standards is your desired end result, and well-designed learning activities are the means to get there. Think of your class as the stair step to your students' next level. If your students develop gaps in their learning, they won't be prepared for the next grade or level of learning, and you will have done them a disservice. Don't get so caught up in your classroom activities that you lose focus on the outcomes of the activities. Examine the purpose behind your activities to ensure that they are clearly aligned to what students should be learning. Remember, activities are not the curriculum.

Examine the purpose behind your activities to ensure that they are clearly aligned to what students should be learning.

YOUR INSTRUCTIONAL BLUEPRINT ■

Using State and District Standards

These days, state and district standards define the curriculum. Standards describe what your students are supposed to know and be able to do as a result of your teaching. Standards are meant to be a guide that ensures that students receive a consistent education based on high expectations and a focus on results. For more information about standards, see the sidebar on page 54 titled "What Are Standards?" The next section, "Moving From the Big Picture to Daily Lesson Plans," explains a four-step process for designing curriculum with standards in mind.

What Are Standards?

Standards are the learning expectations for students completing a grade or course of learning in school. Standards are usually expressed as benchmark skills—concepts and strategies that have been determined for specific grade levels. Standards provide a means of determining the information and skills students should learn, and they assist educators in guiding instruction and assessment.

What is the difference between the curriculum and the standards? Your curriculum is based on the standards. It is basically the blueprint, or plan, for carrying out the standards. It also includes the tools that you will use to provide instruction and is evaluated through your assessment (discussed in Chapter 4).

First Week Flag

Adopted Curriculum

One of the first things you should do when you arrive at your school is get clarification on the district's or school's adopted curriculum. You can get this information by talking to your site administrator or fellow teachers. Getting this information as quickly as possible will give you a good head start on your curriculum planning.

Moving From the Big Picture to Daily Lesson Plans

Start with the "big picture," or blueprint, for learning and organize the information into an appropriate teaching and learning sequence. The diagram in Figure 3.2 outlines four major steps for identifying the curriculum that you will teach on a daily basis.

Figure 3.2   The Curriculum Planning Process

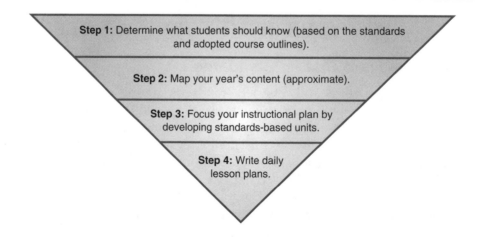

Step 1: Determine what students should know (based on the standards and adopted course outlines).

Step 2: Map your year's content (approximate).

Step 3: Focus your instructional plan by developing standards-based units.

Step 4: Write daily lesson plans.

STEP 1: DETERMINE ■
WHAT STUDENTS SHOULD KNOW

The first step in curriculum planning is to clearly determine your learning targets: those things your students should know and be able to do by the end of the year. You can find these learning targets by examining the standards or adopted objectives of your state and district. These standards give you the direction you need to design your curriculum. If you haven't already received a copy of your standards, be sure to ask your administrator these questions: What are the adopted standards of this district? What am I expected to teach?

─ **Worthwhile Web Sites** ─

Many districts post their standards on their Web sites. This makes it easy to see curriculum connections and to see how your grade level or course content serves as a stepping stone between the previous year or course and those that follow. In addition, the Web offers access to most states' offices of education. To find your state's standards, go to Standards Search at www.statestandards.com.

In addition to standards, most middle and high schools create specific course outlines that are adopted by school boards. Outlines typically exist for all courses and define specific course objectives and instructional content, including sample activities. Many also recommend certain assessment tools and textbooks. You must follow the prescribed course outlines, although you may use activities that are different from the examples listed.

STEP 2: MAP YOUR YEAR'S CONTENT ■

Your list of standards probably looks like an endless list of disjointed skills, concepts, and strategies. Teaching each standard in isolation, one after another, not only would take longer than the traditional school year but also would do little to help students integrate and apply knowledge in any meaningful way. Use the list of isolated objectives and blend them into meaningful units and lessons that advance your students' knowledge and skill base. An easy way to approach this task is to think of your curriculum as a road map that takes your students from one level of knowledge to the desired end result. You may be fortunate to be working

─ **Worthwhile Web Sites** ─

Many Web sites offer ideas for unit and lesson planning. In most cases, these lesson plans and resources are coupled to state educational standards.

AOL@School (www.aolatschool.com)

Education World (www.educationworld.com)

Home2School.com (www.home2school.com)

Microsoft Education Connection (www.k12.msn.com)

in a school that has already developed curriculum maps for each grade level or course. If not, you can create your own map by following this process:

1. *Begin writing your year's plan on a calendar.* Place key events on the calendar, including holidays, breaks and vacations, semesters or trimesters, state and district testing, open house or curriculum nights, final exams, and so on.

2. *Photocopy and cut out each standard.* Use these as puzzle pieces that can be arranged to create a curriculum picture. See the sidebar "Questions to Ask When Examining Standards." (You may prefer to write each standard on a sticky note instead.)

3. *Examine your standards.* Look for standards that are closely connected or redundant. (For example, both language arts and social science may require students to write a research paper.) Group or cluster these standards. Clip these standards together (or write them on the same sticky note). If you are teaching multiple subjects (a typical situation in an elementary setting) or are participating in multidisciplinary teaming, use this process to look for natural connections and opportunities to integrate content areas. In addition, remember to include any schoolwide foci on particular skills, such as problem solving or writing.

4. *Sequence your puzzle pieces into major chunks of time or grading periods.* Begin by clustering standards by trimesters, quarters, semesters, or months. Pay special attention to skills that build on each other throughout the year.

5. *Check for any repetitions or gaps that might affect students' ability to learn the necessary skills.* Repetitions or gaps may be difficult to see at first. However, as you teach your students, you may find that certain steps are repeated or missing. For example, you may ask your students to write a comparison-contrast paper and then find they need more direct instruction on the skills that allow them to do so effectively.

This mapping process is a highly effective vehicle for targeting skills in an integrated fashion. Your school may even use schoolwide curriculum mapping (Jacobs, 1999), in which grade level, course, or department teams determine the sequence and pacing of the curriculum that is taught throughout the year.

Questions to Ask When Examining Standards

➤ What skills and strategies should be learned sequentially?

➤ Are there natural connections between some of the standards in two or more content areas?

➤ Do certain critical activities dictate when specific skills are taught? (For example, if your students are required to take annual writing examinations, then before the exams, you must provide instruction and practice in the types of writing that will be assessed.)

■ **STEP 3: FOCUS YOUR INSTRUCTIONAL PLAN BY DEVELOPING STANDARDS-BASED UNITS**

The third step in creating a curriculum is developing standards-based units. Integrated units provide a structure for delivering content in meaningful clusters. An integrated unit includes a number of standards that can be taught together in a meaningful way. When you cluster related standards under a rich, overarching concept or theme, you not only teach more efficiently, but you also guide your students beyond basic knowledge and literal comprehension and into higher levels of critical thinking, such as application and evaluation. Aim to create and implement three or four major integrated units during the year. (You need not package all your instruction into neat units.)

You have already begun to create integrated units by mapping and looking for natural connections among the standards. Continue this process by reinforcing key skills, using backward planning, organizing your unit, and collaborating with colleagues.

Reinforcing Key Skills

Content standards help determine what you must teach your students. However, you must also teach related skills that may be embedded in a subject or unit. For example, if you teach history, the history standards will guide the majority of your instruction, but you must also teach related skills that may be embedded in the history unit. These skills not only reinforce the learning of history but also provide students an opportunity to practice and apply key skills in a meaningful context. If you integrate key standards and skills across various content areas, you will find that you not only use your teaching time more efficiently; you also help students practice applying skills that are difficult to learn in isolation.

> **Writing can be integrated into many subjects, including mathematics, science, and history or social science classes.**

Begin to integrate key standards and skills by examining standards in other subjects or by talking with colleagues in other departments. For example, writing can be integrated into many subjects, including mathematics, science, and history or social science classes. When approaching a subject, consider the types of writing you can incorporate into that unit. Perhaps the language arts standards at your grade level indicate that your students need to write persuasive letters. You may ask students to write a letter to a historical figure that seeks to persuade the figure to reconsider his or her actions. Imagine the impact of writing this type of persuasive letter rather than merely writing a persuasive letter to satisfy a requirement. This exercise allows students to demonstrate their understanding of the historical figure's role in history, *and* it refines their writing skills. Figure 3.3 provides more examples of standards that can be integrated productively in various ways.

Using Backward Planning

Whether you are planning your instructional units alone or with your colleagues, you will want to use a process that ensures that the units meet your teaching objective. Well-designed, integrated, standards-based units achieve all the following:

- Address identified standards
- Use driving questions or problems to motivate students and focus your instruction
- Include a culminating task that allows students to demonstrate the standards and address the guiding or essential questions or problems

Table 3.1   Skills Connected to Bloom's Taxonomy

Competency	Skills That Demonstrate Competency
Knowledge	Recalling dates, events, places Knowing major concepts and ideas Mastering subject matter
Comprehension	Translating knowledge into a new context Interpreting facts Comparing and contrasting Predicting Summarizing
Application	Using information to solve problems Using methods or concepts in new situations
Analysis	Recognizing patterns Organizing small parts into big ideas Finding hidden meanings
Synthesis	Using old ideas to create new ones Generalizing from given facts Relating knowledge from several areas Drawing conclusions
Evaluation	Comparing and discriminating between points of view Making choices based on reasoned argument

Collaborating With Colleagues: Two (or More) Heads Are Better Than One

The development of instructional units is complex. Yet, when planning is done effectively, it culminates in a useful blueprint for your teaching. When you have planned well-designed units, you no longer need to guess about your next steps for instruction. You have outlined all the steps necessary for students to get from the starting point to the desired results. In fact, because you have worked out the details in advance and planned your instructional sequence, you will actually save yourself time on a daily basis.

Because the process of designing instructional units is complex, you may consider working with your grade-level team or another teaching partner to develop units. Typically, collaboration results in a more quickly developed, higher-quality product because more thinking power is involved in the process.

Finding Time for Collaboration

Where do you find time to work with your colleagues to create or refine units? Opportunities for collaboration vary from school to school. Some schools embed formal planning time into the teaching day, and you can use this time to meet with colleagues. Other schools allow 30 minutes each week for planning, and you can use this opportunity to meet with fellow teachers. Some schools do not provide time for planning, so you and your colleagues must meet after or before school. Chapter 9 presents other ideas for working and learning with your colleagues.

Figure 3.5   Template for Organizing an Integrated Unit

Targeted Standards (What knowledge, skills, and concepts do I want my students to possess? Remember, these may come from several areas of the curriculum.)

Big Idea or Overarching Concept (that unifies the standards)

Prerequisite Skills

Guiding or Driving Question

How Will My Students Demonstrate Their Learning? (What are the performance indicators of success? How will I assess their learning?)

Embedded Curriculum (What else will my students need to do to be successful in this unit? What study skills, thinking skills, and personal skills will they need?)

What Learning Activities Do I Need to Provide?

   Introductory Activities

   Teaching Strategies

   Learning Strategies

   Grouping Strategies

   Evaluation, Presentation, Feedback

   Resources or Tools (including technology)

   Modifications (for advanced learners, English learners, or special needs students)

Figure 3.6   Sample Unit Plan

Targeted Standards (What knowledge, skills, and concepts do I want my students to possess? Remember, these may come from several areas of the curriculum.)

- Identify structural patterns—comparison and contrast, cause and effect, sequential or chronological order, proposition and support—found in informational text to strengthen comprehension.
- Create multi-paragraph compositions.
- Use traditional structures for conveying information (e.g., chronological order, cause and effect, similarity and difference, question and answer).
- Write compositions that describe and explain familiar objects, events, and experiences.
- Discuss the major nations of Native Americans in California. Include their geographic distribution, economic activities, legends, and religious beliefs.

Big Idea or Overarching Concept (that unifies the standards)

- The development of civilization is influenced by a number of factors.

Prerequisite Skills

- Paragraph construction
- Basic Web search

Guiding or Driving Question

- How do the environment and other factors influence the beliefs of a civilization?

How Will My Students Demonstrate Their Learning? (What are the performance indicators of success? How will I assess their learning?)

- Learning teams will create a historical "tour" or overview of a specific tribe of Indians that includes a timeline of the tribe's development, beliefs, cultures, and economic activities.
- Students will write a multi-paragraph essay that discusses their tribe's adaptations to its environment.

Embedded Curriculum (What else will my students need to do to be successful in this unit? What study skills, thinking skills, and personal skills will they need?)

- Research skills: Web search, reading text, developing note cards
- Summarization and organization

What Learning Activities Do I Need to Provide?

Introductory Activities

- Brainstorm about things that affect our culture today. Review timeline and key events in this time period.

Teaching Strategies

- Use direct instruction to teach key research activities and to explain the structure of multi-paragraph essays.

Learning Strategies

- Practice taking notes and organizing research. Create a classroom timeline of tribal development. Examine parallel issues in cultures of today; examine cause-and-effect relationships between environment and beliefs.

Grouping Strategies

- Form collaborative groups for "tribe tour." Involve the whole class in introductory activities.

Evaluation, Presentation, Feedback

- Use rubrics to evaluate tribe tour and civilization-influence paper. Use peer feedback to do a preliminary evaluation of the paper. Teacher evaluates final paper.

Resources or Tools (including technology)

- Use these tools: Internet, word processing, books, artifacts, various California history resources, a local tribal contact.

Modifications (for advanced learners, English learners, or special needs students)

- Encourage partner reading. Use a graphic organizer (web) to depict influences on civilization. Allow students to listen to stories and tests on tape. Employ concept drawing and other direct teaching of concepts and vocabulary.

STEP 4: WRITE DAILY LESSON PLANS ■

Now that you have mapped your year's curriculum and created unit plans, you can follow a fairly straightforward process to develop your daily lesson plans. While writing daily lesson plans may seem tedious at times, you must develop the habit of writing daily plans. Writing lesson plans ensures that you thoughtfully prepare for your students' learning experiences and that you are ready to have a substitute in your classroom should you ever need to be absent. Set aside the same time every week to write lesson plans.

> While writing daily lesson plans may seem tedious at times, you must develop the habit of writing daily plans.

You may choose from a variety of ways to record your lesson plans. In fact, throughout your first year of teaching, you may experiment with different formats until you arrive at one that meets your needs. You may select from a number of commercially produced lesson plan books (available through teacher supply and office product stores). You may create your own template, photocopy it, and place the copies in a three-ring binder. Using your own template saves time in the long run because it is customized to your bell or recess schedule and any other scheduled daily, weekly, or monthly activities. If you aren't interested in creating your own template, you can choose a computer lesson program to create, write, adapt, and save your lesson plans. Whatever format you use, be sure your lesson plans are readily available on your desk for reference by you, your substitute, or your administrator.

Begin creating lesson plans by determining the prescribed instructional minutes for each area of the curriculum that you teach. You can find these guidelines in district policies and state curriculum documents. Your administrator should be able to advise you regarding this information. Use the outline of these instructional minutes to create a basic skeleton for your weekly and daily lesson plans. If you are an elementary teacher, you must plan for a number of subjects. If you are a secondary teacher, you must consider the amount of time allowed for each period. (Most secondary schools follow a traditional schedule, with periods of approximately 55 minutes.) See the sidebar "Teaching in a Block Schedule" for information about block scheduling.

Teaching in a Block Schedule

More and more secondary schools around the country are rethinking student schedules. Schools have modified the traditional schedule—55-minute classes that meet five times each week—to a schedule that allows for larger blocks of learning time. Block schedules vary. Some schools use a 2-hour, rotating block. (For example, students may have six traditional class periods on Mondays and 2-hour block periods on the remaining days. Therefore, students attend periods one, three, and five on Tuesdays and Thursdays and periods two, four, and six on Wednesdays and Fridays.) The key to block scheduling is effectively using the blocks of time. Too often, teachers don't take advantage of the longer learning block and fail to implement active learning strategies. (For more information on active learning strategies, see Chapter 6.)

Be sure to determine times when special activities or groups take students from the classroom. Some students may leave for music instruction or special services during the day (e.g., resource room assistance, speech therapy). Block out these activities in your plans. Avoid scheduling

Figure 3.7   Sample Weekly Schedule for an Elementary Classroom

Time	Monday	Tuesday	Wednesday	Thursday	Friday
8:00–8:10	Opening activities: calendar, lunch count, schedule, review for the day	Opening activities: calendar, lunch count, schedule, review for the day	Opening activities: calendar, lunch count, schedule, review for the day	Opening activities: calendar, lunch count, schedule, review for the day	Opening activities: calendar, lunch count, schedule, review for the day
8:10–9:30	Language arts block: guided reading, shared reading, word study	Language arts block: guided reading, shared reading, word study	Language arts block: guided reading, shared reading, word study	Language arts block: guided reading, shared reading, word study	Language arts block: guided reading, shared reading, word study
9:30–10:00	Daily oral language (DOL) and handwriting	Music	DOL and handwriting	Music	DOL and handwriting
10:00–10:20	Recess	Recess	Recess	Recess	Recess
10:20–10:40	Sustained silent reading (SSR)	SSR	SSR	SSR	SSR
10:40–11:15	Writer's workshop	Writer's workshop	Writer's workshop	Writer's workshop	Writer's workshop
11:15–11:30	Read aloud	Read aloud	Read aloud	Read aloud	Read aloud
11:30–12:10	Lunch and recess	Lunch and recess	Lunch and recess	Lunch and recess	Lunch and recess
12:10–1:00	Math	Math	Math	Math	Math
1:00–1:20	Recess	Recess	Recess	Recess	Recess
1:20–1:55	Social studies and science	PE	Social studies and science	PE	Social studies and science
1:55–2:00	Get our act together (GOAT) time	GOAT time	GOAT time	GOAT time	GOAT time

key lessons, assessments, or critical activities during these times. Figure 3.7 shows a sample weekly schedule for an elementary classroom.

The most common tools you'll use when making your lesson plans are your curriculum maps or long-range plans, your unit plans, and your teacher's editions of textbooks. These tools contribute to the effective integration of your instructional goals, the pacing of your instruction, the content of your activities, and extensions to your lessons.

Typically, you will write a week's lessons at a time. You will revise these lessons each day, depending on the progress you made during the day. Take time to revise lessons immediately after the day ends, when the day's events are still fresh in your memory. You may choose to carry sticky notes and a pen so that you can jot down ideas and notes throughout the day and place these notes in your lesson-planning book.

Thinking It Through: Guidelines for Quality Lessons

You can never do too much planning and preparation for your lessons. The best way to ensure a successful lesson is to really think about the

Brain Bits: Brain-Based Lessons

Many researchers are examining brain research and interpreting its implications for teaching and learning (Sousa, 2006; Wolfe, 2001). The following strategies incorporate the findings of brain research and help you design effective lessons:

➤ *Use a hook.* Grab your students' attention by using some type of emotional hook. Hooks engage the student's limbic system and help the student become alert and interested in learning.

➤ *Connect to previous learning.* Memory is greatly enhanced when new information is connected to prior learning. You can trigger prior learning by reviewing the previous day's lesson. You can also use KWL charts (defined in Chapter 4), metaphors, analogies, and simulations to help your students make meaning of the information they are learning and apply it to their previous learning.

➤ *Help students discover patterns.* The brain naturally seeks out patterns and connections. You can help your students discover patterns and make connections by using graphic organizers, timelines, and other tools that highlight similarities, differences, and connections between information.

➤ *Provide opportunities for reflection.* Learning is strengthened when the brain activates information repeatedly. By reflecting on learning through writing or cooperative learning activities, students reactivate the areas of the brain where the information is stored and strengthen connections in the brain.

➤ *Promote application and transfer.* Students need opportunities to apply new information they have learned in a variety of contexts.

➤ *Actively engage the student.* Students who are actively engaged in learning activities understand new concepts more readily and remember them more effectively. Use active learning strategies, rather than lecturing, to stimulate students' learning.

sequence of events that will take place during your allotted time frame. Planning sequences will become more automatic once you use the planning structure a few times. Use the outline of critical questions shown in Figure 3.8 to plan and prepare effective lessons.

How Can You Promote Active Learning?

You can design activities that foster students' engagement or active involvement in their own learning. Research shows that active learning enhances how quickly students learn and remember new information (Sousa, 2006). Following are common active learning strategies:

➤ *Brainstorming.* Ask individuals or groups of students to list possible solutions to a problem, determine causes and effects, complete KWL charts, or write summaries.

(Continued)

> (Continued)

> ➤ *Group Problem Solving.* Give students difficult or complex problems—such as a real-world math problem—and ask them to work together to find the answer. You may ask groups to make a presentation of their solution to the entire class.

> ➤ *Working Hands On.* Encourage students to complete experiments, construct visual representations of key concepts, or work with manipulatives to solve problems or construct new learning.

> ➤ *Reflecting, Organizing, Interpreting, and Communicating.* Ask students to write journals, participate in group memory activities, complete graphic organizers, or engage in note taking.

> ➤ *Responding Physically.* Have students create human graphs to represent their opinions about an issue, move to different parts of the room to indicate their answers to a multiple-choice question, or line up in the front of the room to represent the parts of speech in a sentence.

> You can use an endless variety of strategies to promote your students' active engagement in learning. Expand your own repertoire of active learning strategies by brainstorming ideas with fellow teachers or by seeking information through books and educational Web sites.

Figure 3.8   Planning and Preparing Effective Lessons

Instructional Goal and Performance Objective(s). What is the goal of the lesson and how will I know that I have achieved it?

Lesson Content. What specifically am I to teach?
Materials. What do I need to have on hand while teaching this lesson? What materials will students need and how will they get them?

Instructional Procedures

1. *Focusing Event.* How will I grab students' attention?

2. *Teaching Procedures.* What methods will I use to teach the information?

3. *Guided Practice.* How will I provide feedback to the students to ensure that they are practicing a new skill correctly?

4. *Progress Checks.* How will I check for student understanding? What type of feedback will I provide to clarify misconceptions?

5. *Student Engagement.* What type of participation do I expect from the students, and how will I get them to participate? How will students transition into each part of the lesson?

6. *Closure.* How will I end the lesson and get students set for the next lesson?

Grouping. What is the most effective way to organize my students for learning? Should students work in pairs, triads, or larger groups? Do my activities match my grouping approach?

Practice and Homework Assignments. What opportunities for extension, practice, and application would be meaningful and beneficial for my students? What type of communication is appropriate with parents regarding these activities?

Adaptations for Students With Unique Learning Needs. What modifications or adaptations might be needed for students who have limited background information or prerequisite skills related to this unit? What resources are available to assist my planning for these students? Are there strategies that would benefit all students while also meeting individual needs?

Fast or Slow: Pacing Lessons

Pacing your instruction is not an exact science. However, you can use the following guidelines to help you determine how quickly to move through your lessons:

- *Establish key skills prior to moving on.* Look at your students and monitor their feedback. Determine their current level of understanding using quick assessment probes. The key is to closely monitor student understanding and remain flexible in your daily plans to accommodate necessary changes. If students do not receive enough practice with double-digit multiplication, they won't be equipped to move on to triple-digit multiplication. If students struggle with passages in their literature book, rethink your selections for independent reading.
- *Consider the amount of time the textbook allows for the instruction of the concepts.* Textbooks are typically field-tested by other teachers and should serve as effective instructional pacing guides.
- *Talk to your fellow teachers.* They can suggest how much time it takes to teach certain concepts.

A LAST LOOK AT THE TEACHER AS A DESIGNER OF INSTRUCTION

Designing appropriate and effective instruction is a complex task. This critical process provides students with instruction that is aligned with requisite standards and tailored to meet their needs. As you incorporate the strategies you have learned in this chapter, you will refine your curriculum over time. Remember, the process of curriculum design is ongoing. By working with others and planning one piece at a time, you will develop your curriculum in a manageable fashion. Your students will reap the benefits, and you will love the results.

Worthwhile Web Sites

Here are a few of the Web sites that offer resources for lesson and unit planning:

Blue Web'n (www.kn.pacbell.com/wired/bluewebn)

ERIC Lesson Plans
(www.eduref.org/Virtual/Lessons/)

Lesson Plans Page.com (www.lessonplanspage.com)

■ RECOMMENDED READINGS

Harris, D., & Carr, J. (1996). *How to use standards in the classroom*. Alexandria, VA: Association for Supervision and Curriculum Development.

Jacobs, H. H. (1989). *Interdisciplinary curriculum: Design and implementation*. Alexandria, VA: Association for Supervision and Curriculum Development.

Marzano, R. J., Pickering, D., & Pollock, J. (2001). *Classroom instruction that works: Research-based strategies for increasing student achievement*. Alexandria, VA: Association for Supervision and Curriculum Development.

Rominger, L., Heisinger, K., & Elkin, N. (2001). *Your first year as an elementary school teacher: Making the transition from total novice to a successful professional*. Roseville, CA: Prima.

Rominger, L., Laughrea, S., & Elkin, N. (2001). *Your first year as a high school teacher: Making the transition from total novice to a successful professional*. Roseville, CA: Prima.

Strong, R. W., Silver, H. F., & Perini, M. J. (2001). *Teaching what matters most*. Alexandria, VA: Association for Supervision and Curriculum Development.

Wiggins, G., & McTighe, J. (1998). *Understanding by design*. Alexandria, VA: Association for Supervision and Curriculum Development.

Questions for Reflection

What areas of my curriculum present the biggest challenge?

_____

_____

_____

_____

_____

How have I organized my curriculum?

_____

_____

_____

_____

_____

_____

What strategies can I use to ensure that what happens in my class is aligned with what the students are expected to know and do?

_____

_____

_____

_____

_____

_____

Teacher as an Assessor

"HOW DO I KNOW THEY ARE LEARNING?"

If you were engaged in a word association game and the first word presented was *candy,* you might respond with the word *chocolate.* If the next word was *bright,* you might say *light.* And chances are, if you are like most people, when you hear the word *assessment,* you immediately think of the word *test.* In fact, reading the title of this chapter may have elevated your anxiety level. Be assured, however, that this chapter is designed to reprogram your reaction to the word *assessment.*

> **Think of assessment as a tool that can assist you in a variety of ways to positively affect student learning in your classroom.**

Assessment is one of the most critical and helpful aspects of teaching. In fact, the word *assess* is derived from the same Latin root as the word *assist.* From now on, think of assessment as a tool that can assist you in a variety of ways to positively affect student learning in your classroom. You will learn how to use assessments to gauge whether or not your students

- Are ready to learn
- Grasp the new concepts you are teaching
- Can integrate and apply these concepts in different situations
- Can demonstrate your targeted outcomes (e.g., concepts, skills, and strategies) by the end of the course or unit

■ WHAT IS ASSESSMENT?

The subject of assessment is complex. Assessment is often misperceived or becomes tangled with other issues. We can begin talking about assessment by clarifying what assessment is and what it is not.

- Assessment is ongoing.
- Assessment should trigger a response.
- Assessment is not grading.
- Assessment is multifaceted.

Assessment Is Ongoing

Most professionals use some type of assessment to inform their work on an ongoing basis. Yet, far too often, teachers rely only on limited feedback, such as standardized tests administered once or twice yearly or major tests given at the end of a semester. As a teacher and a professional, consider taking the same approach as a physician: Check your students' learning at regular intervals. Think of assessment as a tool that threads throughout your entire teaching process instead of a monster that pounces at the end of a unit or a semester. Monitor your students' learning with assessment tools that answer these questions:

> **Check your students' learning at regular intervals.**

- To what extent do my students already possess these skills and concepts?
- What background knowledge and skills do my students have that will assist them in learning new skills and concepts?
- Do my students understand the concepts as they are engaging in the learning activities that I have designed and implemented?
- Can my students demonstrate these skills and this knowledge in a meaningful way?

Assessment Should Trigger a Response

Assessment is not a one-way street; it should elicit feedback. Effective assessment provides feedback to you and your students. Use this feedback to determine how you might adjust your teaching pace or content, to identify individuals or groups of students who may be struggling, and to reinforce challenging concepts. Provide ongoing feedback to students so that they are aware of their own levels of achievement and performance. Help students focus on the key information they need to learn and apply as well as any areas in which they need to improve.

Assessment Is Not Grading

While this chapter will examine some issues related to grading, assessment and grading should not be confused. Assessment means gaining information about your students' progress toward learning specific skills, concepts, and strategies (i.e., do they understand?). Assessment is a dynamic function of good teaching that informs your instruction and helps guide you to improved student learning. On the other hand, grading assigns values to students' levels of performance (i.e., how well do they understand?). Grading is a static indicator of the end result.

> Assessment is a dynamic function of good teaching.

Assessment Is Multifaceted

Effective classroom assessment is complex: it looks different from classroom to classroom and from teacher to teacher. If you wish to gain adequate information about your students' learning, you must develop a number of assessment strategies based on what you teach and on the needs and abilities of your students. You must use a range of informal and formal assessments before, during, and after your instruction. With experience and the support of your colleagues, you can begin to construct an assessment tool kit from which you can choose appropriate measures of student learning.

THREE PHASES OF ASSESSMENT: DIAGNOSTIC, FORMATIVE, AND SUMMATIVE

In Chapter 3, you determined your curriculum—what students should know and be able to do. Now you must decide how you will recognize (assess) whether or not students attain the knowledge and skills outlined in your curriculum. What evidence indicates that your students attained the skills, concepts, and understandings targeted by your instruction? What type of assessment is needed to determine whether students attained these skills, concepts, and understandings?

The learning process encompasses three phases of assessment—diagnostic (pre-instruction), formative (ongoing), and summative (culminating). These phases are summarized in Figure 4.1 and are fully explained in the following paragraphs. Use the guiding questions to help you remember the purpose for each assessment phase. Notice the multiple assessment options listed for each phase. These assessments help you determine whether your students are ready to learn, grasping new concepts, mastering certain skills, and assimilating broad ideas in a meaningful and useful way. Some of the assessment options are informal while others are formal. All are designed to provide feedback that you can use to modify and improve your instruction. The examples are not exhaustive.

> **All assessment options are designed to provide feedback that you can use to modify and improve your instruction.**

Figure 4.1   Three Phases of Classroom Assessment

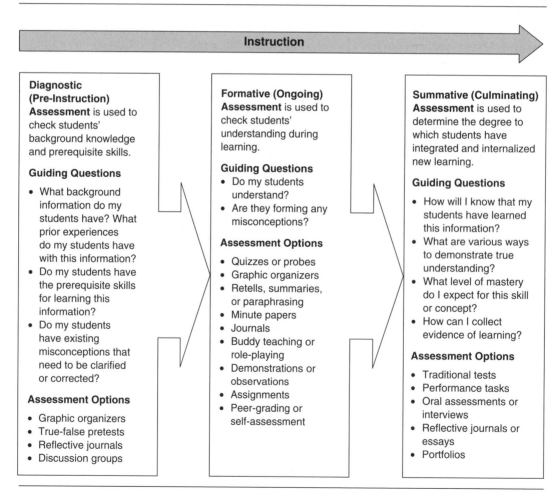

Instruction

Diagnostic (Pre-Instruction) Assessment is used to check students' background knowledge and prerequisite skills.

Guiding Questions

- What background information do my students have? What prior experiences do my students have with this information?
- Do my students have the prerequisite skills for learning this information?
- Do my students have existing misconceptions that need to be clarified or corrected?

Assessment Options

- Graphic organizers
- True-false pretests
- Reflective journals
- Discussion groups

Formative (Ongoing) Assessment is used to check students' understanding during learning.

Guiding Questions

- Do my students understand?
- Are they forming any misconceptions?

Assessment Options

- Quizzes or probes
- Graphic organizers
- Retells, summaries, or paraphrasing
- Minute papers
- Journals
- Buddy teaching or role-playing
- Demonstrations or observations
- Assignments
- Peer-grading or self-assessment

Summative (Culminating) Assessment is used to determine the degree to which students have integrated and internalized new learning.

Guiding Questions

- How will I know that my students have learned this information?
- What are various ways to demonstrate true understanding?
- What level of mastery do I expect for this skill or concept?
- How can I collect evidence of learning?

Assessment Options

- Traditional tests
- Performance tasks
- Oral assessments or interviews
- Reflective journals or essays
- Portfolios

Typically, within a unit of instruction, you will use several forms of assessment, each with a different purpose and context.

Diagnostic (Pre-Instruction) Assessment

One of the most critical steps in assessment happens before you teach. Your goal in diagnostic (pre-instruction) assessment is to find out what your students already know compared with what you want them to learn. Use this phase to determine students' knowledge of related concepts and skills and how you might help students make associations between these concepts and skills on the one hand and the new information on the other. By figuring out your students' background knowledge, you will gain valuable insights into how to organize your instruction, what concepts you must reinforce, and what misconceptions you may need to undo. In addition, you can prepare students for new information by reinforcing previous learning and refreshing their background knowledge.

You may choose from a variety of diagnostic (pre-instruction) assessments, including graphic organizers, true-false pretests, reflective journals, and discussion groups.

Graphic Organizers

Graphic organizers offer a number of ways to determine students' prior knowledge and understanding of new concepts. You may ask students to use a Venn diagram to demonstrate their understanding of relationships between concepts, events, or other significant information. You may tell them to keep a copy of the Venn diagram and later compare it with another version.

Another type of graphic organizer that lends itself well to this phase of assessment is the KWL chart (Ogle, 1986; the initials *K*, *W*, and *L* are explained below). The KWL uses a multiphase approach that helps students (a) access their prior knowledge, (b) generate guiding questions about the topic they will be studying, and (c) record new learning on completion of the unit or area of study. To use a KWL, ask students to draw a three-column chart (see Figure 4.2). Tell students to write what they already *know* about a topic in the K column and what they *want* to know in the W column. This will give you an idea of their level of understanding of a particular concept or topic, as well as areas that they find unclear or intriguing. After your instruction about the topic, ask students to complete the L column to determine what they *learned* (KWL is discussed in more detail below). You can use KWL charts with a whole class or with small groups of students. (Note: See the discussion of graphic organizers later in this chapter. You can modify these organizers and use them as pre-instruction assessments.)

True-False Pretests

Conduct a quick check of students' background knowledge with a true-false test. Ask students to indicate their responses on paper or signal with a thumbs up or a thumbs down sign. Use this approach to gain insight into students' perceptions, interpretations of events, knowledge, and skills.

Figure 4.2   KWL Chart

What Do We KNOW About _____?	What Do We WANT to Know About _____?	What Have We LEARNED About _____?

Reflective Journals

Challenge students to quickly write all they know about a topic related to an upcoming unit of instruction. Reflective journal entries can be a more personal version of the KWL, in which students write what they know and what they want to know about the topic.

Discussion Groups

Encourage students to work in teams to develop theories and discuss background knowledge and related concepts. Ask the groups to then summarize their discussion. Team members can present their summaries to the rest of the class in a number of ways, including oral presentations or graphic representations of ideas. Asking students to work in teams not only helps them establish student background knowledge but also sets the tone for team learning. See the sidebar titled "KWL in Context" for an example of how to combine KWL with a discussion group to assess students' prior knowledge and encourage students' acquisition of new knowledge.

Formative (Ongoing) Assessment

Unfortunately, teachers often wait until their instruction is complete before checking their students' progress toward mastery of key skills or understanding of major concepts in the unit. They fail to check whether their instruction is working and whether the students understand. If these teachers administer a final exam for the unit and discover that students haven't understood, then the students have not benefited from the instruction.

KWL in Context

Mr. DiCaprio was all set to teach his unit on the Civil War. He divided his class into three learning teams and challenged each team to complete a KWL chart on one aspect of the period. One group focused on economic issues, another on social issues, and the last on political issues. Each group brainstormed what they knew (K) regarding their particular aspect of the Civil War. In addition, they developed guiding questions—what they wanted to know (W)—which they could use to frame their exploration of content throughout the unit. After groups completed the K and W columns, they shared their information and posted their charts on the wall.

From this information Mr. DiCaprio was able to determine the prior knowledge he could build on and the areas that might require less focus. In addition, as a result of having completed the activity, the students now had an advance organizer that would help them classify their new learning.

Don't wait until the end of teaching to determine whether your instructional methods are working. Teachers must check periodically that their instruction is effective. This type of assessment is called formative (ongoing) assessment. Formative (ongoing) assessments help you gather information as you teach. Use the data collected from formative assessments to answer these questions:

> **Teachers must check periodically that their instruction is effective.**

- Do I need to reteach some of the information?
- Does a group of students need additional teaching and practice?
- Is my pacing appropriate?
- Are students missing some foundational skills?
- Are my students engaged in this learning? Do I need to find other ways to make my teaching more active and motivating?
- Do I need to spend more time helping students transfer their skills? (In other words, are students able to transfer their learning?)

First Week Flag

Gather Information on Your Students' Abilities, Strengths, Weaknesses, and Interests

The first week of school is a great time to begin gathering information on your students' abilities, strengths, weaknesses, and interests. You can use a variety of tools to gather this information, such as reading inventories, vocabulary activities, interest surveys, journal writing, and skill probes. Be sure to review the information found in the students' cumulative files so that you can determine what special needs you will be addressing in your classroom. Build a file of possible assessments prior to the first day of school and use them as sponge activities while you are interviewing or working with small groups of students.

You can monitor your students' understanding through a variety of formative assessments, including quizzes or probes; graphic organizers; retells, summaries, or paraphrasing; minute papers; journals; buddy teaching or role-playing; demonstrations or observations; assignments; and peer grading or self-assessment.

Quizzes or Probes

Use quizzes (probes) to check students' acquisition of basic skills and common facts. You can include multiple-choice, short-answer, true-false, and fill-in-the-blank questions on quizzes. Quizzes are generally easy to review and provide students with helpful feedback regarding their knowledge of facts and operations. You may use a quiz to help students recall the seven continents, certain constitutional amendments, or math facts.

As you grade the quizzes, keep a tally of incorrect answers. Use this tally to determine how well students grasp the concepts and foundational skills they need prior to applying the skills.

> Students can use graphic organizers to sequence activities or events, to demonstrate relationships, and to compare and contrast information, or track newly acquired knowledge while they are engaged in learning activities.

Graphic Organizers

Students can use graphic organizers to sequence activities or events (e.g., timelines, pictures, boxes), to demonstrate relationships (e.g., Venn diagrams, concept webs), and to compare and contrast information (e.g., charts with sections for "How Alike" and "How Different") or track newly acquired knowledge (e.g., by means of a KWL chart) while they are engaged in learning activities. Students who have difficulty writing can use a graphic organizer as a starting point for writing. When you use graphic organizers in the diagnostic (pre-instruction) phase and the formative (ongoing) phase, you can ask students to compare the organizers to reflect on their new learning.

Retells, Summaries, or Paraphrases

Brain research supports the fact that individuals truly integrate information when they communicate new ideas or concepts to others (see Brain Bits). Therefore, retelling, summarizing, and paraphrasing are effective ways to assess whether your students comprehend what you have taught them. When students state an idea in their own words, you can determine whether the students truly understand concepts or events and are able to explain them to others. Examining your students' ability to summarize, retell, or paraphrase allows you to observe the degree to which they are synthesizing new information. Students can do retells, summaries, or paraphrases in oral or written form. You may ask younger students to orally summarize the events in a story or a scientific experiment. You can even ask students to paraphrase key concepts, events, and information to their peers in pairs or small groups. Through this process, students will hear information repeated, which serves to reinforce and assist their memories.

Brain Bits

Brain research has discovered a strong relationship between rehearsal and memory (Wagner et al., 1998). When the brain learns new information, it forms new connections between neurons. The cells surrounding the connections produce a special protein. This protein strengthens the pathway and points the way to the neural connection the next time the individual encounters the information. Each time the pathway processes the information, it is strengthened, and the brain works more efficiently. When students tell others about the information they've learned—in either oral or written form—they strengthen the neural pathways in their brains, increasing the likelihood that the information will be stored in long-term memory. Therefore, it is beneficial to use retells, summaries, and paraphrasing in your learning activities.

Minute Papers

You can ask students to write minute papers to demonstrate what they've learned. Minute papers are written responses to a series of questions:

- What was the most important thing you learned in class today?
- What questions do you have about what we are learning?
- What is still confusing?

Examining students' responses to these questions will give you tremendous information regarding students' understanding of the concepts and skills you presented in your instruction.

Journals

Journals are a powerful way to gain insight into students' understanding and perceptions of new information. There are two key guidelines for using journals to assess student understanding:

1. *Clearly identify the purpose for journaling.* In other words, don't ask students to journal just to journal. Be sure to have a reason and focus for asking students to write in their journals.

2. *Examine student journals on a timely and regular basis.* Students want to know that their writing interests you. They will be more likely to provide you with good information if they see that you use the information to plan your instructional responses.

Table 4.1 highlights the types of journals available for classrooms. Each type has a different focus and set of benefits. The journal types are explained in the following paragraphs.

- *Reflective journals* allow students to reflect on information they have recently heard, read, or observed and record the key ideas, connect to previous learning, or make predictions about cause-and-effect relationships. Students can also use reflective journals to explain the thinking processes they used to solve problems, organize information, or locate resources about a particular topic or content area.

- *Interactive journals or learning logs* are a very effective way to monitor student learning on a continuous basis. Interactive journals allow you to ask questions of students and hold ongoing conversations about their learning.

- *Buddy journals* allow pairs of students the opportunity to write back and forth to each other about the content they are learning. You can guide conversations by posing questions, or you can allow students to generate their own questions and conversational topics.

- *Reader response or dialogue journals* allow you to emphasize the meaning of text while providing natural, functional experiences in both writing and reading. Ask students to divide their journal pages into two columns. Tell them to write quotations from the text in one column and their responses and reactions to those quotations in the other column.

- *Skill journals* provide a place for students to demonstrate various problem-solving skills (e.g., mathematics operations) and to describe the process they used to solve problems.

Table 4.1   Journal Types

Type of Journal	Focus	Benefits
Reflective journals	• Reflecting on information • Recording key ideas • Connecting to previous learning • Making predictions about cause-and-effect relationships • Explaining thinking processes	• Provide a specific time and place to personalize learning • Help strengthen memory of the information
Interactive journals or learning logs	• Monitoring learning • Asking questions • Creating ongoing conversations	• Provide students with tangible evidence of their teacher's interest in their learning • Provide teachers with a quick snapshot of student understanding • Reinforce the "writing as communicating" concept • Give students models of good responses by means of the teacher's responses
Buddy journals	• Engaging in ongoing conversations about content	• Foster relationships between students
Reader response or dialogue journals	• Responding to narrative or informational text	• Strengthen reading comprehension by requiring students to actively dialogue or interact with the text • Create a reading log that students can refer to at a later date • Provide a safe place to express opinions, interpretations, and perspectives
Skill journals	• Summarizing and demonstrating skills and concepts	• Generate a quick snapshot of student understanding considerate of the learning of others. • Offer a place to practice and demonstrate new skills • Reinforce newly learned procedures (This type of journal is ideal for mathematics.)

Buddy Teaching or Role-Playing

Buddy teaching (or role-playing) is similar to retelling, summarizing, or paraphrasing. Through enacting or teaching a new concept or skill for another student, students consolidate and reinforce learning, not only for the other student, but also for themselves. Students generally enjoy these exchanges and can give feedback on each other's ability to share the information in a logical, succinct fashion. This strategy is particularly effective with mathematical operations; however, be certain that you have checked students' ability to do the operations correctly before you ask them to teach others.

Demonstrations or Observations

Demonstrations (or observations) allow you to check each student's understanding of a foundational skill (e.g., regrouping in mathematics or reading passages from a guided reading book). Ask each student to do an individual demonstration of the skill for you. Considering the problems that could arise if a student continues to perform the skill in the wrong way, spending 1–2 minutes for each demonstration is time well spent. Use the demonstration time to correct a student's misconceptions or procedural errors before they become ingrained in the student's thinking. If several students seem to struggle with the same misconceptions, cluster these students into a group and give them some additional teaching in key skills.

Be sure to create a record-keeping system to collect this data. You may create *a class list and matrix of subject-specific skills* or use an existing observational checklist. Use the matrix or checklist to quickly code each student's proficiency in the skills. You may choose to use a *sticky note system* rather than a matrix or checklist. As you observe each student, jot down a couple of notes on a sticky note and put the note in your grade book for later recording. If you strive to complete a sticky note for each student by the end of each week, you will collect a great deal of assessment information.

Assignments

Used wisely, assignments are not only a useful tool for reinforcing your instruction; they can also provide you with much information about how well students are grasping new concepts or applying new skills and strategies. Again, be sure to analyze student responses and uncover misconceptions. Use this information to refocus or adjust your teaching.

Peer Grading and Self-Assessment

Peer grading and self-assessment are two of the most valuable learning experiences students can have. Using answer keys, rubrics, and examples of quality work, students can grade each other's work during class time or give each other constructive feedback on various projects. As students interact with correct answers, rubrics, and exemplars, their learning and the expectations for quality performance are naturally reinforced. As a result, students examine their own work with a more critical eye. You will also benefit by having them use peer grading and self-assessment because you will spend less time grading simple assignments and will have more time to grade more substantive assignments.

Summative (Culminating) Assessment

Frequently, teachers use end-of-chapter or unit tests to determine how much students have learned during an instructional unit. These tests typically assume the form of a traditional multiple-choice or essay examination. However, summative assessment need not happen merely at the end of a chapter or unit. Instead, evidence of student achievement may be gathered throughout the unit, and this evidence may be presented as a project, a research paper, or other performance task at the end of the unit.

The following paragraphs describe a variety of summative (culminating) assessments for measuring students' understanding of major units of study. These assessments include traditional tests, performance tasks, oral assessments or interviews, reflective journals or essays, and portfolios.

Traditional Tests

One of the most common ways to assess student learning is by using traditional tests. Most often, traditional tests are designed in true-false, multiple-choice, fill-in-the-blank, matching, or short-answer formats. These formats are generally objective and easy to score and leave little room for interpretation. Many teachers have students use electronic, scannable answer forms, which allow the teachers to score a large number of tests in a very short time.

┌─ **Thinking Skills in Bloom's Taxonomy**

➤ Remembering
➤ Understanding
➤ Applying
➤ Analyzing
➤ Evaluating
➤ Creating

The key to whether these tests are beneficial to you as a teacher is how they are designed. Figure 4.3 outlines ways to ensure that your tests allow you to collect useful information.

In general, traditional tests can be used effectively to determine whether students can recall information and key facts. However, their value is limited in tapping the higher-level thinking skills of Bloom's taxonomy (analyzing, evaluating, and creating; see the sidebar "Thinking Skills in Bloom's Taxonomy"). In addition, your students possess a variety of learning styles and may not truly demonstrate their knowledge through traditional testing. Therefore, you will most likely want to explore assessment options other than traditional testing.

Performance Tasks

Students often ask, how is this going to help me later in life? Performance tasks can help students find answers to this question. Performance tasks, as opposed to traditional tests, integrate the application of skills into real-life or authentic tasks. Performance tasks allow students to demonstrate a deeper understanding of what they know than they can by merely answering multiple-choice questions. Effectively designed performance tasks measure whether your students are meeting your targeted objectives and allow students to choose tasks according to their interests and strengths. When students choose their tasks, they are highly motivated and eager to engage in performance measures. In fact, you will often see

Figure 4.3   Getting the Most From Traditional Tests

True-False Tests

Instead of merely asking students to respond with a T or an F, challenge them to explain their F answers. Explaining their answers not only gives students opportunities to write but also allows them to demonstrate their thinking processes and gives you insights into their understanding of the subject matter.

Multiple-Choice Tests

When writing multiple-choice questions, make sure that your wording is clear. Be certain that your answers match the verb tenses in the questions. Avoid wordiness (lengthy questions or answers), and limit the number of choices to four. Review the choices for each question to be sure that only one choice is correct. Ask yourself whether the difficulty level of the questions is reasonable for your students.

Fill-in-the-Blank Tests

Use this format when you want students to recall key facts or phrases. Be sure to use blanks that are equal in length so that students don't identify the correct word based on size.

Tests With Matching

Tests involving matching can be useful to measure students' recollection of factual information or to discriminate between concepts. Be sure to design the test with consistency within each matching set. For example, if you are asking students to match key events in one column to dates in another, don't confuse sides. Help students distinguish between prompts (or stems) and responses by numbering one side and labeling the other side with letters. Try to keep all items on the same page to avoid confusion. Provide more answers than prompts so students cannot merely use the process of elimination.

Short-Answer Tests

Short-answer tests can probe students' understanding of new concepts and knowledge quickly. Be sure to provide clear directions for responses. For example, will you require that students write in complete sentences, or will you accept fragments?

Performance Tasks in Action

➤ *Science.* As a culminating activity to a unit in environmental science, students examined a company's land use proposal, identified possible environmental-impact questions, and developed a written response to the company that requested specific information.

➤ *Math.* Following a unit on fractions, students developed a menu for an upcoming class party and created a shopping list. (They were given single-serving recipes as a starting point.)

➤ *Social Science.* Students assumed the role of a Southern landowner just before the Civil War and responded to the slavery issue by writing a letter to President Lincoln.

➤ *Language Arts.* After a unit on evaluation of media, students created political campaigns, including Web sites, newspaper articles, and television commercials.

students' best work emerge as a result of their participation in a performance assessment. Some sample performance tasks are described in the "Performance Tasks in Action" sidebar.

> ## Backward Planning
>
> The term *backward planning* is used throughout this book. Remember, backward planning is a universal strategy that can be applied when designing your curriculum, your assessments, and your instructional strategies. It requires that you *begin with the end in mind* rather than designing your instruction without clear learning targets. By using backward planning, you'll ensure that all your learning activities, including assessment, are directly connected to the outcomes or goals you have targeted for your students' learning. As a result of using backward planning, you will always have a clear answer for the question, why am I doing this?

> ## What Is a Rubric?
>
> How good is good enough? Rubrics are effective tools for answering that question for students, parents—and even you. A *rubric* is a tool that defines the criteria or expectations of a learning task and assigns values to each level of quality. Rubrics can be used to assess student performance in a number of learning tasks and can even be used as teaching tools (Andrade, 2000). Rubrics are a clear and easy way to communicate not only the "what" of a learning task but also the "how" and "how well." Think of a rubric as an advance organizer for students—a way of getting feedback before they even begin their project or task. It can even serve as an organizer for your own teaching.

The performance task may focus on a particular skill (e.g., constructing a well-organized paragraph) or may integrate multiple skills and concepts. Regardless of the format or scope, the defining characteristic of a performance task is that it involves the authentic application or performance of the targeted learning in a meaningful context.

Design your performance task before beginning your instruction.

Design your performance task before beginning your instruction. Use backward planning to (a) determine what standards you will address in your instruction, (b) choose the big concepts you will teach, and (c) formulate guiding questions that will shape the content and design of your instruction. Once you have figured out what your students will be learning, you can determine what authentic products they could create to demonstrate that they understand.

Do not confuse performance tasks with projects. While students do enjoy projects, only projects designed to measure student achievement of standards are truly performance tasks. If performance tasks are to function as effective assessment tools, they must have a clearly defined purpose and target specific learning outcomes. However, obtaining clear assessment information from performance tasks can be difficult because performance tasks are complicated and varied. The best tool you can use to clearly define the expectations and information you seek in a performance task is a rubric (see the "What Is a Rubric?" sidebar).

Oral Assessments or Interviews

Oral assessments or interviews can be used as alternatives to paper-and-pencil tests or other measures. Oral assessments offer an opportunity for students to reflect on their learning and demonstrate that they have gained the knowledge and concepts you have targeted in your instruction. This is a particularly effective approach for students who have difficulty expressing their ideas in writing. When you use oral assessments or interviews, be certain to develop a rubric to assist your evaluation of student knowledge.

Reflective Journals or Essays

Reflective journals and essays provide useful information regarding students' true understanding of concepts. However, if you wish to use journals or essays as effective assessment tools, be sure to develop a rubric of your expectations. First, decide what skills or concepts you'll be targeting. Second, define the criteria for demonstrating these skills or concepts. Be sure to explain the skills, concepts, and criteria prior to assigning the task so that students have a clear understanding of the purpose and the quality expectations for their journal or essay responses.

Portfolios

A portfolio is a collection of student work that serves as evidence of learning a specific set of skills and concepts throughout a particular time. If a portfolio is to serve as an effective assessment tool, its purpose and structure must be clarified from the beginning. Following are common types of portfolios:

- *Writing portfolios* include a variety of writing samples collected throughout a year or years.
- *Quality, or "best work," portfolios* include materials that students have chosen because they believe the materials demonstrate their highest-quality work.
- *Unit portfolios* show work from a study of specific concepts or topics within a content area (e.g., a geology unit or a unit on World War I).
- *Standards portfolios* demonstrate evidence of meeting the standards.

Take time to determine the requirements for what should be included in the portfolio, outline a time frame for submitting artifacts, and designate overall expectations for quality. Your expectations may be highly rigorous or very flexible, depending on the purpose and context of the portfolio. However, you must establish a rubric to guide students in the development of a portfolio and to provide you with a structured framework for evaluating the portfolio.

RUBRICS ■

Throughout the explanations of each type of assessment, the word *rubric* has reappeared over and over. Rubrics are mentioned so often because they are tools that take the "guessing out of assessing." We can use rubrics to clarify the expectations for content and quality whether we are assessing performance tasks, oral assessments, interviews, reflective journals, essays, or portfolios. In general, a rubric is a scale that outlines a range of performance levels and assigns a value to each level. Typically, teachers design four-level rubrics. Four-level rubrics describe performances that exceed standards, meet standards, minimally meet standards, or do not meet standards. You can create rubrics for a number of assignments and tasks, such as research papers, projects, and demonstrations. You may choose to create the rubrics yourself, or you may create rubrics in collaboration with students. (Collaborating with students to create rubrics is an especially powerful learning tool.)

Benefits of Rubrics

Rubrics are immensely helpful because they provide focus for your students. Use rubrics to give your students a preview of your expectations. Clarify the goals, guidelines, and standards for the product via the rubric. When students are given rubrics *before* they begin a task, they better understand what is being asked of them and they have a clearer sense of purpose in their work.

Rubrics also help sharpen your teaching. As you develop each rubric, you will constantly examine your standards. This ensures that you design tasks that truly assess student learning. When you develop a rubric prior to your instruction and the assignment, you ensure that you create a solid connection between the learning task and its purpose for gathering evidence of learning in your classroom. Too often teachers create performance tasks that are merely projects. These tasks have little connection to what students need to know and do and offer scant information regarding the degree to which students have learned the skills, strategies, and concepts that are targeted in the standards.

Developing rubrics can be time consuming, but in the end, rubrics ensure consistency of assessment, clarity of desired outcomes, and communication of expectations to your students. Rubrics are appropriate for any performance task—essays, research papers, role-playing, and so on. You will be amazed at how well your students perform when they are given a rubric prior to developing their papers or projects. When students know what you want, they will strive to accomplish it.

Teacher-Developed Rubrics

While at first glance rubrics may seem complex, they are relatively simple to create. Figure 4.4 lists the steps in creating a four-level instructional rubric. An explanation of each of the steps follows.

Step 1: Analyze the Task and Determine Which Components to Score

Group your criteria into several areas and determine a variety of perspectives from which you will assess student performance. Here are some sample performance tasks and their possible components:

- *Speech.* Organization, delivery, content, appeal
- *Research Paper.* Content, research process, organization, format

- *Demonstration.* Research, organization, materials, delivery, summary or conclusions
- *Investigation.* Procedures, findings or content, application of previously learned information, summary

Figure 4.4   Steps for Developing a Four-Level Rubric

1. Analyze the task and determine which components to score.

2. Determine what it looks like to meet the standard.

3. Write a draft rubric for meeting the standard.

4. Repeat Steps 2 and 3 for (a) exceeding the standard, (b) partially meeting the standard, and (c) not meeting the standard. Write a draft rubric for exceeding, partially meeting, and not meeting the standard.

5. Assign descriptors to each level (optional).

Step 2: Determine What It Looks Like to Meet the Standard

Use a number of resources to assist you in this step, including work by previous years' students, specific performance standards available from your district or state, and input from your colleagues. List the qualities that appear in a performance that meets the standards. Create an overall description of what it takes to demonstrate that a student is meeting the standard. Use this description as level three in your four-level rubric.

Step 3: Write a Draft Rubric for Meeting the Standard

Use words that specifically describe how the performance should look. Be sure to integrate all the standards that are examined through the performance task and address each aspect or component of the task. Include the factors that set apart a performance that meets the standards from a performance that partially meets the standards. (See Figure 4.5 for examples of language to describe these factors.)

Step 4: Repeat Steps 2 and 3 for (a) Exceeding the Standard, (b) Partially Meeting the Standard, and (c) Not Meeting the Standard

Write a draft rubric for exceeding, partially meeting, and not meeting the standard. (Figure 4.5 also provides examples of language to describe these levels.)

Step 5: Assign Descriptors to Each Level (Optional)

Instead of merely using a numeral for each level, you may choose to use words such as "You are there!" or "On target!"

When you follow these steps, you will end up with a rubric similar to the sample shown in Figure 4.5. This sample was designed to assess student research papers. This rubric is an effective tool for both teaching the requirements of effective research papers and evaluating student research papers.

Figure 4.5   Sample Rubric: Preparation and Presentation of a Report

	Wow!	Nicely Done!	Getting There . . .	Needs Improvement
Content	Demonstrated thorough understanding of key concepts and used clear examples to illustrate to the reader.	Demonstrated accurate understanding of key concepts.	Demonstrated incomplete understanding of important concepts and had minor misconceptions.	Demonstrated significant misconceptions about the concepts and information.
Organization of Information	Clearly synthesized extensive amounts of information into a logical and understandable document for the reader.	Provided effective organization, sequence, and summary of the information obtained through research.	Attempted to organize information, but sequence somewhat difficult to follow.	Little or no attempt to organize information for the reader.
Research Process	Extensive evidence of multiple sources of information, including primary source documents, interviews, etc.	Significant evidence of multiple sources of information, including primary source documents.	Some evidence of multiple sources of information.	No evidence of multiple sources of information.
Format	Highly effective and creative use of writing conventions, graphics, and formatting to gain attention of the resder.	Writing conventions were followed; use of graphics assisted explanation of concepts.	Minor errors in writing conventions; minimal use of graphics to assist the reader.	Several writing convention errors and ineffective use of graphics.

Student-Generated Rubrics

While the rubrics you design as a teacher are valuable, student-generated rubrics are an even more powerful learning tool.

Begin by asking students to examine the standards with you. Show standards on an overhead, highlighting those that will be addressed within the unit.

Next, use the five-step process used in creating teacher-generated rubrics (see Figure 4.4 and the discussion above). Facilitate a dialogue with your class to identify how student work should look when it (a) exceeds the standard, (b) meets the standard, (c) partially meets the standard, and (d) does not meet the standard. Show students examples of projects or papers that meet or exceed the standards. These examples will help students determine how a project should look in order to meet the standards.

By engaging in this rubric-making process, your students will gain a clear understanding of your expectations as well as the process of assessing their performance. Creating rubrics also prepares students to offer feedback to their peers as they complete their tasks.

■ EXEMPLARS AND ANCHOR PAPERS

One of the most powerful things you can provide your students is a good example of student work. By sharing *exemplars* or *anchor papers* (samples of proficiency) with your students, you empower students with tangible evidence of work that meets or exceeds the standards. Collect exemplars and anchor papers from adopted materials and text or from former students. Some states provide these on their Web sites or in print.

A number of excellent models are available for teachers to use while designing performance tasks. Many are available in professional books on the subject. See the Recommended Readings at the end of this chapter.

Worthwhile Web Sites

These sites offer great free resources for designing quizzes, rubrics, and checklists:

Educator's Reference Desk (www.eduref.org)

Teachnology (www.teach-nology.com/web_tools/rubrics)

Web for Teachers (www.4teachers.org)

Several educational vendors offer CD-ROM or Web-based programs to assist with the development of rubrics, exemplars, and anchor papers. Here are some of these resources, in addition to Teachnology (listed above):

Exemplars (www.exemplars.com)

Rubistar (rubistar.4teachers.org)

Rubric Builder (landmark-project.com/rubric_builder/index.php)

COMMUNICATING ASSESSMENT INFORMATION ■

Throughout your instruction, your feedback to students assists their learning. Be sure that the feedback is useful and leads to increased learning. If you merely mark essays with comments such as "Great!" or "You can do better!" you fail to provide information that assists students' growth and learning. Strive to be specific in your comments. Guide students in how to improve by making comments such as "I particularly liked it when you used descriptive language as you developed the character, but I need you to use more supporting details to justify your answer." Specific comments come across as objective and serve to minimize students' sense that they are being personally attacked when they receive less than stellar grades.

> **Strive to be specific in your comments.**

You should provide feedback on all assignments, but you do not necessarily need to grade each piece. Remember, the idea of assignments is to provide you and the student with formative assessment information about how the student is learning the concepts throughout your instruction. While students must be held accountable for completing their work, they should not be penalized for incorrect answers while they are learning concepts.

(Continued)

Avoid Grading on a Curve

Grading on a curve involves ranking students according to their level of performance and then assigning grades to each percentage of students. For example, the highest 20% of students may receive an A, the next 20% of students may receive a B, and so on. This practice not only results in students' competing against each other for grades but communicates the notion that no matter how well students achieve, there will always be the same number of A's, B's, C's, and so on. The practice of grading on a curve is incompatible with your goal that all students demonstrate understanding of the concepts and skills outlined by the standards. Instead of grading on a curve, base your grades on meeting specific standards rather than on comparing students with other students.

┌─ Worthwhile Web Sites ───────

The following Web sites are great resources for electronic grading:

E-Z Grader (www.ezgrader.com/)

Grade Machine (www.mistycity.com)

Electronic Grading Systems

If you wish to create frequent, informal progress reports, consider using a Web-based or electronic reporting system. Many electronic grading systems are available to help teachers manage assignments and grades (see Worthwhile Web Sites above). Some of these systems are Web based, which allows the information to be viewed by parents and students. Check with your school or district to see if one of these systems is available for your use.

┌─ Testing Challenges ───────

Two key areas affect students' ability to perform well on high-stakes achievement tests. Both are related to literacy: reading for comprehension and writing on demand.

First, students must be able to read for sustained amounts of time with adequate comprehension. Quite frequently on these tests, and particularly at higher grade levels, students are required to read long passages of information and apply comprehension strategies in order to respond correctly. This reading requirement can be found within any content area, such as history, language arts, or mathematics. If students cannot accurately comprehend a word problem, they will not understand which operation or strategy to use to determine an accurate answer. In this day of sound bites and quick Web searches, students are not exposed to reading for sustained periods of time. Therefore, you must use strategies to embed this skill in your activities. Give students opportunities to practice responding to various levels of comprehension questions after they read passages. (See Chapter 5 for ideas for building your students' reading comprehension.)

Second, students must be able to write on demand. In an on-demand writing test, students read a passage and are asked to respond in writing to a prompt or sentence stem. This task differs greatly from traditional writing activities, in which students choose a topic and spend several days working through the typical writing process. Students who can write well in the traditional format may struggle with on-demand writing tests because of the structure, time constraints, and limited focus of the writing prompt. To prepare your students for successful on-demand writing, scaffold these skills across the year by teaching specific strategies for responding to writing prompts. Check to see whether your state offers sample prompts and rubrics for assessing student answers, and use these samples with your students. Ask your testing coordinator or site administrator for further information regarding your state's high-stakes testing. Here are more ideas for helping your students prepare for standardized tests:

➤ *Review your assessment results and curriculum.* Be sure there are no significant gaps or differences between what students are expected to know and what you are teaching.

➤ *Design some of your classroom probes and quizzes to have the same format as standardized tests.* You might expose your students to various formats by embedding them in your sponge activities at the beginning of the period or at certain times during the week.

➤ *Provide students with sample responses,* and discuss how each is scored and why each is scored in a particular way.

➤ *Give students practice in oral and written comprehension strategies,* such as finding the most relevant information or main idea, summarizing, and comparing and contrasting. Be sure to use a variety of contexts for this practice, including word problems in math as well as science or social studies passages.

➤ *Review mathematical and scientific numerals, symbols, and terms.*

➤ *Guide students in how to review their work.* Show them how to use strategies such as estimating and rechecking.

➤ *Teach students to use graphic organizers* when responding to writing prompts.

STANDARDIZED TESTING ■

Most states and districts now require regular standardized testing to ensure that students are demonstrating achievement of the standards. Statewide assessments are considered to be "high stakes" because they directly affect school funding and ratings. Some states require that students pass exit exams before they receive their diplomas. In certain states, high-stakes tests are criterion referenced, which means that students need to reach a certain level of competency in order to pass. Other states use norm-referenced tests, which means that students' scores are compared to a representative sample of students in the same grade. Scores from this type of test are usually provided in the form of percentile ranking.

In general, if the tests are aligned to your content standards, then your standards-based instruction will assist students in preparing for these high-stakes tests. However, students not only need content knowledge to pass the tests; they also need test-taking skills so that they can represent their knowledge accurately on the test. Students who are unfamiliar with test formats often become flustered with a new variation and perform poorly even when they know the content information being tested. For example, many second-grade students are never exposed to "bubble in" answer sheets or multiple-choice questions with "none of the above" or "all of the above" as choices. Vary your tests to expose your students to these test formats. Textbook publishers can often supply tests demonstrating various testing formats. Obtain preparation materials prior to the testing period and take time to review them with students. Be sure to gather as much information as you can about your state's high-stakes testing, and be sure to work with your administrator to understand your responsibilities for preparing your students.

■ A LAST LOOK AT THE TEACHER AS AN ASSESSOR

Assessment can powerfully assist your instructional program. Following are keys to successful assessment in the classroom:

• *Assessment and instruction are linked.* They should not be treated as separate events.

• *Your assessment must be driven by your targeted learning outcomes, which are based on your content standards.* Regardless of which assessment tools you use, you must focus on your learning standards and establish clear expectations prior to your instruction.

• *Each type of assessment is suited to different purposes and will give you different information.* Use a combination of assessments to gauge your students' learning.

• *To truly assist you as you teach your students, your assessment system must provide ongoing information about how your students are progressing.* In other words, assessment takes place at all times—not just at the end of an instructional unit.

• *Avoid creating a complicated assessment system because a complicated system can overwhelm your teaching.* Examine your system to see if it can be simplified. Share your system with others to get feedback and new ideas.

• *At the beginning and throughout instruction, inform students about how you will gather information about their learning.* Give feedback on a regular basis. Involve students in developing rubrics, analyzing their own and others' work, and examining exemplars.

• *Remember that assessment has many forms and purposes.* Be a good consumer of assessment data. Know what the purpose and design of each assessment is and what the information truly means in terms of your teaching.

• *Finally, give yourself time to incorporate all aspects of a total assessment program.* Whether you're a developing teacher or a veteran, continually reflect on and revise your assessment process.

RECOMMENDED READINGS ■

Burke, K. (2005). *How to assess authentic learning* (4th ed.). Thousand Oaks, CA: Corwin Press.

Guskey, T. R., & Bailey, J. M. (2001). *Developing grading and reporting systems for student learning: Experts in assessment.* Thousand Oaks, CA: Corwin Press.

Lazear, D. (1994). *Multiple intelligence approaches to assessment.* Tucson, AZ: Zephyr.

Lewin, L., & Shoemaker, B. (1998). *Great performances: Creating classroom-based assessment tasks.* Alexandria, VA: Association for Supervision and Curriculum Development.

Mitchell, R., Crawford, M., & Chicago Teachers Union Quest Center. (1995). *Learning in overdrive: Designing curriculum, instruction, and assessment from standards.* Golden, CO: Fulcrum Resources.

Stiggins, R. (2001). *Student-involved classroom assessment* (3rd ed.). Upper Saddle River, NJ: Merrill Prentice Hall.

Wiggins, G., & McTighe, J. (1998). *Understanding by design.* Alexandria, VA: Association for Supervision and Curriculum Development.

Questions for Reflection

How have I embedded the three main phases of assessment into my instructional program?

_____

_____

_____

_____

_____

_____

In what area of assessment would I like to become more effective?

_____

_____

_____

_____

_____

_____

What resources can I use to help refine my assessment process in this area?

_____

_____

_____

_____

_____

_____

5

Teacher as a Promoter of Literacy

Basics of Reading
- Understanding Concepts of Print
- Gaining Phonemic Awareness
- Understanding and Using Phonics
- Recognizing Sight Words
- Developing Automaticity
- Expanding Vocabulary
- Increasing Background Knowledge
- Monitoring Comprehension

Beginning With the End in Mind
- What Is the Difference Between a Skill and a Strategy?
- Comprehension Strategies

Moving From Learning to Read to Reading to Learn
- Before-Reading Strategies
- During-Reading Strategies
- After-Reading Strategies

Determining Reading Levels

Using Lexiles to Determine Reading Levels
- How Are Lexiles Determined?
- What Does a Lexile Level Tell About What a Student Can Read?
- How Do I Find the Lexile Level of a Book?

(Continued)

(Continued)

Promoting Independent Reading
- What Research Says About Independent Reading
- How to Begin an Independent Reading Program

Creating a Classroom Library

Working With Struggling Readers: Designing an Intervention Program

Reading Aloud to Students
- How to Recognize a Good Read-Aloud Book

Encouraging Parents to Participate in Their Child's Reading

Assessing Reading Comprehension

A Last Look at the Teacher as a Promoter of Literacy

Recommended Readings

Questions for Reflection

"HOW DO I HELP MY STUDENTS BECOME STRONG READERS AND WRITERS?"

Whether you are a kindergarten or a twelfth-grade teacher, if you teach any subject, you are expected to be a reading teacher. This task is daunting for many, especially content specialists who never thought they would be responsible for teaching reading. However, after learning a few basics of reading instruction and better understanding the reading process, all teachers can help their students strengthen their literacy skills. No matter what subject you teach, you will quickly surmise that if your students can't read their textbooks, they will have difficulty learning in your class.

■ BASICS OF READING

Learning to read is a process. For some students, the reading process happens naturally and with ease, but other students struggle to master this critical skill. Strong readers conquer the two main stages of reading: decoding and comprehending. First, readers must learn to decode words—convert print into the spoken form. Second, readers must be able to comprehend what they read. Figure 5.1 shows the skills and strategies students conquer as they learn to read well. Each of the skills and strategies is further explained in the paragraphs that follow. (These terms and many others are also defined in Figure 5.8, Glossary of Reading Terms, at the end of this chapter.)

The Reading Process
- ➤ *Step 1.* Decode
- ➤ *Step 2.* Comprehend

Figure 5.1   Learning to Read: A Progression of Skills and Strategies

1. Understanding concepts of print

2. Gaining phonemic awareness

3. Understanding and using phonics

4. Recognizing sight words

5. Developing automaticity

6. Expanding vocabulary

7. Increasing background knowledge

8. Monitoring comprehension

Understanding Concepts of Print

The first step in learning to read English is understanding concepts of print. From an early age, children begin to learn what a book is and how it is used. Students must understand a number of concepts of print in order to learn to read:

- Students must realize that print carries a message.
- Students must understand that print comes in many forms.
- Students must recognize that print corresponds to speech, word for word.
- Students must understand how stories work.
- Students must develop concepts about spacing, words, and word boundaries.
- Students must recognize the differences between letters and words.
- Students must understand the parts of a book.
- Students must realize that print has directionality; that is, we read print from left to right, top to bottom, and front to back.

Gaining Phonemic Awareness

The second step in learning to read is gaining phonemic awareness. Students understand that every spoken word is made up of a sequence of phonemes, or speech sounds. They learn to use the following techniques as they gain phonemic awareness:

- *Blending sounds* (/k/ /u/ /p/ = cup)
- *Segmenting sounds* (What sounds make up the word *cup*?)
- *Manipulating phonemes* ("Say *clap* without the /k/." "Lap.")

Understanding and Using Phonics

The third step in learning to read is understanding and using phonics. Students learn that symbols have corresponding sounds, and they apply these sound-symbol relationships in order to read words. Students develop phonics knowledge when they learn to recognize and name letters.

Recognizing Sight Words

The fourth step in learning to read is recognizing sight words. Students learn to recognize words automatically (on sight) as they become familiar with them. When first exposed to a word, a student must sound it out. However, as the student encounters that word again and again, the connections between the sound and the letters strengthen. Eventually, the spelling of the word is represented as a unit in the student's memory. Many young readers rapidly develop their recognition of frequently occurring sight words.

Developing Automaticity

The fifth step in learning to read is developing automaticity. As students gain the ability to recognize words or series of words, their reading requires less effort. Automaticity—the automatic recognition of words—frees the student's mind to concentrate on the word's meaning in relation to its context. This is a critical step in unlocking meaning for proficient readers.

Expanding Vocabulary

The sixth step in learning to read is expanding vocabulary. As students begin to read more and encounter more words, their vocabulary increases. As students expand their vocabulary, they find it easier to comprehend what they are reading.

Increasing Background Knowledge

The seventh step in learning to read is increasing background knowledge. As students read more and grow older, their background knowledge increases because they have more life experiences as well as reading experiences. Their increased background knowledge allows them to be more active and involved readers and improves their comprehension.

Monitoring Comprehension

The eighth step in learning to read is monitoring comprehension. Students learn to monitor their reading for understanding, and they gain skills and strategies to help themselves when they do not understand what they are reading. For example, students who are monitoring their comprehension might realize when they have become distracted and don't remember what they read. They will reread the text section to be sure they understand it before they move on to the next section.

■ BEGINNING WITH THE END IN MIND

Covey (1990), in *The 7 Habits of Highly Effective People,* says that successful people begin with the end in mind. If we seek to promote literacy, we must begin by knowing the skills and strategies strong readers use most frequently. For many years educators and researchers studied struggling readers for clues about the best way to teach reading. In the early 1990s researchers began to study and identify the reading strategies that strong readers use to comprehend what they are reading. In *Reading Instruction That Works* (2002), author Michael Pressley summarized more than 60 studies that analyzed skilled readers. As researchers and educators identified what proficient readers do, they then explored ways to teach these strategies and skills to all students.

What Is the Difference Between a Skill and a Strategy?

Many teachers use the words *skills* and *strategies* as synonyms although in actuality their meanings are quite different.

- *Skills* are routine, almost automatic, behaviors generally associated with lower levels of thinking and learning. Using skills connotes a passive relationship between the reader and the text; the reader passively receives information from the text. Most of the time, students unconsciously use reading skills without monitoring their use of the skills. For example, students learn the skill of decoding words. This skill includes how to recognize sounds, associate sounds with letters, and eventually automatically recognize letter-sound relationships. Strong readers do not spend their entire lives sounding out words; instead they learn to use decoding skills, memorize the skills, and move on.

- *Strategies* are conscious, flexible plans a reader applies to a variety of narrative and expository texts. Using strategies connotes an active relationship between the reader and the text; the reader uses awareness, reflection, and interaction to actively encounter the text. Most strategies are interrelated and recursive. After students learn decoding skills, they begin to use active strategies to understand what the words are trying to say. Reading evolves from an unconscious act into heightened awareness and reflection.

Comprehension Strategies

In the past decade, many prominent literacy researchers have written about the importance of helping students become strategic readers. Some of these researchers are Michael Pressley (*Reading Instruction That Works*), Stephanie Harvey and Anne Goudvis (*Strategies That Work: Teaching Comprehension to Enhance Understanding*), and Ellen Keene and Susan Zimmermann (*Mosaic of Thought: Teaching Comprehension in a Reader's Workshop*). These and other researchers have identified a variety of comprehension strategies that they feel are important to teach. Table 5.1 provides you with some of the most commonly agreed-on reading comprehension strategies, an explanation for each, and some of the questions good readers ask themselves when using these strategies.

Part of a teacher's job is to help students learn to use comprehension strategies flexibly and decide when they are needed. Good readers don't use a single strategy for a single text or even a single strategy at a time. Students eventually learn to use these strategies in whatever combination

Table 5.1   Reading Comprehension Strategies

Strategy	Explanation	What Good Readers Are Thinking When They Use This Strategy
Connecting	Good readers connect what they know with what they are reading.	• Does this remind me of something? • Has this ever happened to me? • Do I know someone like him or her? • Am I like this character?
Predicting	Good readers think about what is going to happen and make predictions based on what they know and what they have read.	• What do I think will happen next? • Since _____ happened, I think _____ will happen. • While looking over the material before reading, I predict I will learn about _____. • This title or heading or picture makes me think _____.
Questioning	Good readers ask themselves questions when they read.	• What is the author saying? • Why is that happening? • Why do I think this character did _____? • Is this important? • This makes me wonder _____.
Monitoring, clarifying	Good readers stop to think about what they are reading and know what to do when they don't understand.	• Is this making sense? • What have I learned? • Should I slow down? Speed up? • Do I need to reread? • What does this word mean?
Summarizing	Good readers identify the most important ideas and restate them in their own words.	• In my own words, this is about _____. • What do I think is most important? • The author's most important ideas were _____. • What has happened so far in the story?
Visualizing	Good readers picture what is happening while they read.	• What are the pictures in my head? • What do I hear, taste, smell, or feel?
Inferring	Good readers combine clues from what they are reading with what they already know to fill in information not given by the author.	• What text clues can help me fill in missing information? • How can I use what I know to add to what I'm reading? • Although the author hasn't told me this, I think _____.

is needed in a given situation. When you teach students each strategy, be sure to do the following:

- Describe the strategy.
- Give real reasons and examples for applying the strategy. (Take time to model the strategy.)

- Describe when students should apply the strategy.
- Tell students how to use this strategy in coordination with other strategies.
- Show proof that the strategy really works.

Teaching Reading Strategies: Systematic Instruction

The first step in teaching reading strategies is giving explicit and systematic instruction in the strategies. During the past decade, educators and researchers have called for explicit and systematic instruction in all aspects of reading instruction. These educators and researchers realize that many teachers have faulty assumptions about how students learn to read. Some teachers believe students learn to read by simply being exposed to or working with reading concepts. Other teachers assume that if they merely mention concepts, their students will learn them. Still other teachers believe that if students simply participate in reading, they will learn to comprehend what they are reading. For some students, these approaches work and work well. However, to become better readers, most students need direct instruction in reading concepts and strategies. This is especially true for learning phonics and decoding. However, older readers also need direct instruction in comprehension strategies in order to learn how to think critically about what they are reading.

To become better readers, most students need direct instruction in reading concepts and strategies.

To create a balanced and strategic model for teaching literacy, be sure to follow these guidelines:

- Examine the objective to be learned. Then select and sequence the essential skills, examples, and strategies necessary to achieve the objective.
- Allocate sufficient time to learn essential skills.
- Organize information in order to minimize confusion on the part of the learner.
- Introduce information in manageable and sequential units.
- Identify prerequisite skills and build on learners' prior knowledge.
- Review previously taught skills.
- Integrate old knowledge with new knowledge.
- Progress from simpler contexts to more complex contexts.

Teachers must use systematic instruction if they are to build a strong foundation in reading. Right from the start, be sure you know what you are trying to teach, what the students need to learn, and how you can design lessons that strategically point your students in the right direction.

Teaching Reading Strategies: Gradual Release of Responsibility

The second step in teaching reading strategies is using the gradual release of responsibility method (see Figure 5.2). This approach begins with the teacher's taking most of the responsibility by systematically teaching and modeling the strategy. Then the teacher steps back and allows the students to use what they have learned on their own, first in guided practice and then in independent practice. Finally, students apply the strategy

Figure 5.2   Gradual Release of Responsibility Approach

1. *Model the strategy.* Begin by explaining the strategy to your students and demonstrate how to apply the strategy successfully. Use a think-aloud to model the mental process that you use when you apply the strategy. (A think-aloud simply means that you literally think out loud for your students to hear.) By hearing you talking through your thinking process, students learn when and how to use each strategy.

2. *Encourage guided practice.* Gradually give students more responsibility as you practice the strategy with your students. Scaffold the students' attempts and support students' thinking as you give feedback. (Scaffolding means that you organize activities from simplest to most complex. Students experience success in simple activities before they progress to more complex activities.)

3. *Allow time for independent practice.* Encourage students to try the strategy on their own. Be certain to offer ongoing and consistent feedback to students to ensure that they correctly practice the strategy.

4. *Challenge students to apply the strategy.* Once students have mastered the use of the strategy in isolation, they must learn to apply it to a different text or situation. Observing how well students apply their knowledge will help you determine whether they have mastered the strategy. If students have difficulty applying the strategy to other texts or situations, reteach the concept by returning to guided practice.

to a new context. Students gradually assume more and more responsibility for using and mastering the strategy through this approach.

■ MOVING FROM LEARNING TO READ TO READING TO LEARN

Once students leave the primary grades, we hope that they have learned to read so that they can focus their attention on reading to learn. Much of a student's learning from the upper elementary grades onward centers on information and content. Once students leave high school, 90% of their

Increasing Reading Comprehension

Use the following activities to increase students' reading comprehension:

➤ Create real and meaningful reasons for students to read texts.

➤ Choose texts carefully. Match instruction of specific strategies and purposes to appropriate texts.

➤ Provide many opportunities to build vocabulary and word knowledge.

➤ Focus on decoding skills and reading fluency.

➤ Challenge students to regularly engage in writing texts for others to read and comprehend.

➤ Foster an environment in which students and teachers engage in high-quality discussions about what they read.

➤ Use ongoing assessments to determine students' application of comprehension strategies.

reading will be for information and only 10% will be for pleasure (Daggett, 1990). Many teachers devote most of their instructional time to presenting new concepts and very little time teaching students how to read their textbooks and supplemental materials.

We usually assume that upper elementary and secondary students already know how to read a textbook for information. However, we must remember that each textbook is different and that students must be taught how to glean information from their textbooks. Teaching students how to read their textbooks is one of the most empowering things teachers can do for their students. Through systematic instruction, students learn how to enhance their own learning, ultimately taking full responsibility for their learning. Table 5.2 lists many easy-to-use instructional strategies that can help students improve their content reading. Each strategy is explained in the paragraphs that follow.

Table 5.2   Instructional Strategies for Improving Content Reading

Before Reading	*During Reading*	*After Reading*
• Preview the material • Make predictions • Identify unfamiliar vocabulary • Activate background knowledge • Set a purpose for reading	• Monitor understanding • Visualize the content • Make ongoing predictions • Practice self-questioning	• Summarize • Reflect • Write

Before-Reading Strategies

To help students warm up to a text they are about to read, try some of the following strategies.

• *Preview the material.* Teach students to look through the chapter, read the subheadings, and look at maps, graphs, and pictures. Help students realize that they can learn a lot by previewing the material.

• *Make predictions.* Help students predict what they are going to learn when they read the book. Show students the cover of the book and discuss the title to help them get ideas for their predictions.

• *Identify unfamiliar vocabulary.* Define words that students do not know. Help students learn methods for tackling unfamiliar words, such as using other sources for finding the meaning of the words.

• *Activate background knowledge.* Help students recognize what they already know about the subject discussed in the book. Ask students questions and stimulate discussion to help students discover what they already know.

• *Set a purpose for reading.* Ask students to identify why they are reading what they are reading and what they hope to learn from it. Many students might answer that they have no idea why they are reading the material. Your job is to teach students that there is a purpose in reading different materials and that it is important for them to know why they are reading these materials.

During-Reading Strategies

As students read the selected text, try some of the following strategies to increase students' understanding of what they are reading.

- *Monitor understanding.* Help students learn to monitor themselves for understanding and comprehension. Teach them to understand that when they get distracted, they should return to the text and reread it. Encourage students to ask questions of themselves, their peers, or their teachers if they don't comprehend what they are reading. Tell students that they may simply need to slow down their reading in order to understand the content.

- *Visualize the content.* Challenge students to make mental movies when they are reading. Ask them what kind of pictures they see in their mind's eye when they are reading a certain story or part of a text.

- *Make ongoing predictions.* In addition to making predictions before reading the text, students should make predictions while they are reading. Ask students to make predictions about what is going to happen next and why they think it will happen. Teach students to look for clues in the text to help them make their predictions.

- *Practice self-questioning.* Encourage students to ask themselves questions about what they are reading. They might ask themselves questions such as, what is the author trying to say? or what is this character's motive? Teach students different types of questions to use when reading different types of texts. For example, explain that when students read expository text, they should ask themselves questions such as, what is the important idea of this section?

After-Reading Strategies

After students have read the text, try some of the following strategies to help students clarify and solidify their learning.

- *Summarize.* After students read the material, ask them to summarize what they read. Teach them that a summary is a brief overview of the most important details and ideas in the text. Model summarizing for students on a regular basis. Summarizing is not an easy task; students need to be taught and given examples of good summaries.

- *Reflect.* Encourage students to reflect on what they read. Challenge them to ask themselves what they learned and whether their purpose for reading was fulfilled.

- *Write.* Ask students to write about what they read. Writing enhances reading comprehension. Encourage students to write about their opinions or feelings about the text, compare the text with another text, or create a sequel to the story. Check your state standards to see what writing applications are designated for your grade level and concentrate on using these applications with your students.

DETERMINING READING LEVELS ■

Before-, during-, and after-reading strategies greatly enhance students' comprehension of text. However, it is also important to match students' reading abilities to appropriate texts. If a text is mismatched to students' abilities, the students will not be able to comprehend the text no matter how many reading strategies they use. In *Reading Essentials* (2003), Regie Routman described the various levels of text and how they fit each reader.

Text may be divided into three levels:

1. *Just Right Books.* These books seem custom made for the students, and with very little help from an adult, the students can confidently read and understand a text they find interesting.

2. *Easy Reading.* Students can easily read these books. They build confidence and fluency as well as help students focus on meaning in the text. Easy books are critical to help students become successful readers. The only caution here is that students should not read easy books exclusively. Learners need a variety of easy and just right books.

3. *Hard Books.* These books are above the student's comprehension level and can be used instructionally by a teacher who is guiding and facilitating the reading and discussion of the text. Yet when reading one of these books independently, a student can quickly become frustrated. Some students might insist on trying to read a hard book because it relates to their interests. This is fine as long as that student does not have a steady diet of hard books. Teachers quickly find students pretending to read hard books but not really reading or comprehending the text.

USING LEXILES TO DETERMINE ■
READING LEVELS

A powerful way to ensure that students are reading just right books is to use Lexile levels (Schnick & Knickelbine, 2000). A Lexile is a numerical score that indicates the readability of written material and the comprehension level of a reader. Lexile levels range from 0 for beginners to 2000 for postgraduate readers and materials. Lexile levels for readers can often be obtained from commonly used standardized tests. A teacher, media specialist, or parent can approximate the reader's Lexile level by asking what books the reader is currently reading or by asking the reader to read aloud from books with a known Lexile level and noting the student's ease or difficulty in reading the passages.

How Are Lexiles Determined?

Lexiles are determined by using the Lexile Analyzer. In this process, an entire book is scanned and evaluated for word frequency, sentence difficulty, and sentence length. Complex words carry a higher weight in Lexile ranking. Therefore, some picture books, especially those with nonfiction content, may actually have a higher Lexile level than one might expect, due to a high ratio of multisyllabic words to the total number of words in the book.

What Does a Lexile Level Tell About What a Student Can Read?

When a reader has the same Lexile level as a text, the reader is expected to read that text with 75% comprehension. When reader and text measures match, the reader is "targeted." Targeted readers report competence, confidence, and control over the text. (This corresponds to the just right instructional level mentioned previously.) Students reading texts that are 250 Lexile levels above their identified level indicate frustration, inadequacy, and lack of control; comprehension drops to 50%. (This corresponds to the hard reading level mentioned previously.) Students reading texts that are 250 Lexile levels below their identified level experience total control and automaticity, and comprehension rises to 90%. (This corresponds to the easy books level mentioned previously.) The three Lexile levels correspond to the three levels previously mentioned, but the basis for determining Lexile levels is more comprehensive.

How Do I Find the Lexile Level of a Book?

The Lexile Web site has a database of more than 30,000 books and their respective Lexile levels. You can view the Web site free of charge at www.Lexile.com. Many publishers are also beginning to provide Lexile levels for their books.

■ PROMOTING INDEPENDENT READING

For students to learn to become stronger readers, they have to read—a pretty simple, yet very powerful concept. This is bolstered by what Stanovich (1986) has named the Matthew Effect. This phenomenon is based on the "rich-get-richer, poor-get-poorer" concept, in which children who learn to read early read more and become better readers. Children who struggle in reading read less, and consequently, their skills improve at a slower rate.

As a teacher, you cannot afford to ignore or neglect independent reading in your classroom. Independent reading not only helps students become better readers and allows them to comprehend content; it also raises achievement test scores. Table 5.3 presents the striking results of a study that examined the amount of time fifth graders spent reading and its impact on their achievement (Cunningham & Stanovich, 1997).

Additional research shows that independent reading may help students develop positive attitudes toward reading. Independent reading offers a way for students to practice what they have learned in reading lessons and to use and internalize reading strategies. Silent reading helps students interact with text in a low-stress situation. Independent reading also provides reading time for students who are slow readers and who normally have little free time for reading.

Table 5.3   Student Achievement and Independent Reading

Minutes per Day Spent Reading	Student Achievement Test Percentile
90.7	98
40.4	90
21.7	70
12.9	50
3.1	20
1.6	10

SOURCE: Adapted from Cunningham & Stanovich (1997).

What Research Says About Independent Reading

Independent reading is the best practice for learning to read. As in sports and music, practice in reading makes perfect. The single most valuable activity for developing reading comprehension is reading itself. Research indicates that the amount of reading students do is a predictor of growth in reading comprehension. Recent research has yielded the following key findings:

- The amount of independent reading students do predicts the quantity and quality of language use and vocabulary in their writing.
- Through independent reading, students encounter new words, new language, and new facts. They also encounter new ways of thinking that may never arise in their face-to-face worlds. In the interest of their own greatest potential and fulfillment, all students should be encouraged to read frequently, broadly, and thoughtfully.
- Independent reading—more than socioeconomic status or any instructional approach—is the single factor most strongly associated with reading achievement.
- Independent reading predicts the richness of students' oral language.
- Researchers are convinced that reading volume, rather than oral communication, is the prime contributor to individual differences in students' vocabularies.
- The best way to show students that reading is an important activity is to make time for it every day.
- Like adults who read for pleasure, students should know that personal interest is the most important factor in choosing books to read for pleasure.
- It is of paramount importance that students read, regardless of the perceived quality of the literature.

Silent Sustained Reading (SSR) and Drop Everything and Read (DEAR) are the most commonly used names for a defined, uninterrupted amount of time during a selected part of the school day when everyone in a classroom (including the teacher) reads from self-selected books or materials. To have a successful SSR or DEAR session in your classroom, follow these guidelines:

1. *Set a time of day and length of time.* Be consistent; choose certain days of the week and specific times for silent reading. For example, students should know that every day after lunch or every Monday, Wednesday, and Friday after second period, they will have a 15-minute reading time.

2. *Model good reading practices.* Be sure that the classroom is quiet and that students can read without interruptions. Research has found that SSR and DEAR are much more successful when the adult in the room reads right along with the students. Take this time to stay current on children's literature or to brush up on some old classics.

3. *Allow students to self-select their reading materials.* Students need to feel in control of what they read during this time. Allowing students to select their own reading materials is very empowering and motivating. You might need to help a student find a book at an appropriate level, but do your best to give the student a choice between two books so as to provide the experience of self-selection.

4. *Provide freedom from testing and questioning.* Avoid formal testing or questioning regarding students' reading after SSR or DEAR. The purpose of silent reading is to help students enjoy reading for the sake of reading.

First Week Flag

Interest and Reading Inventories

The Student Interest Inventory (Figure 5.3) and the Reading Inventory (Figure 5.4) are excellent activities for the first week of school. Give students time to complete them in class and then to share their answers in small groups and with the class as a whole. These activities will facilitate students' getting to know one another as well as help you ascertain the types of books your students might be most interested in reading.

How to Begin an Independent Reading Program

The following tips provide time-tested advice on how to design a successful independent reading program:

1. *Get information.* Ask students to complete the Student Interest Inventory (Figure 5.3) and the Reading Inventory (Figure 5.4) to help you assess their current independent reading habits as well as help them select books to read.

2. *Teach students the five-finger rule for selecting books.* Tell them to read the first page of the book they are considering. If there are five words on that page that they don't know, then that book is too difficult for them, and they should choose another book.

3. *Select days and times for independent reading.* In addition, explain to students that you will assign independent reading for homework and that

they always need to have something to read on their own.

4. *Establish classroom rules for independent reading.* Help students recognize early on that this time is sacred, quiet, and uninterrupted.

5. *Conduct book shares.* Use the Classroom Book Recommendation List (Figure 5.5) to enable students to recommend books they like. Display the form somewhere in the room where students can contribute to it and read others' comments. Make book discussions and recommendations a natural and common occurrence in your classroom. Feature and display books throughout your classroom.

6. *Motivate students to read.* Provide incentives and recognition for students who read independently. Give bookmarks, coveted classroom jobs, and books as incentives.

Consider purchasing the following reading-related books for your professional library:

➤ Adams, M. J. (1990). *Beginning to read: Thinking and learning about print.* Cambridge, MA: MIT.

➤ Billmeyer, R. (1996). *Teaching reading in the content areas: If not me, then who?* Aurora, CO: Mid-continent Regional Educational Laboratory.

➤ Harvey, S., & Goudvis, A. (2000). *Strategies that work: Teaching comprehension to enhance understanding.* Portland, ME: Stenhouse.

➤ Honig, B. (1996). *Teaching our children to read: The role of skills in a comprehensive reading program.* Thousand Oaks, CA: Corwin Press.

➤ Keene, E., & Zimmermann, S. (1997). *Mosaic of thought: Teaching comprehension in a reader's workshop.* Portsmouth, NH: Heinemann.

➤ Trelease, J. (2001). *The read-aloud handbook.* New York: Penguin.

CREATING A CLASSROOM LIBRARY ■

To help promote widespread and frequent independent reading, create an exciting and up-to-date classroom library. Follow these tips:

• *Assess your library's needs.* Consider the grade level you teach and the types of books that should be in your library. Think about students' interests and reading levels.

• *Learn about children's books.* Visit Web sites, libraries, and bookstores to learn more about the types of books available for students. Read journals and magazines geared toward children's literature.

• *Acquire a core set of books, magazines, and reference materials for your library.* Use book clubs (e.g., Scholastic) to buy more books for your money. Look for inexpensive or free ways to build your book collection. Ask students to donate a "legacy book" in the name of friends, parents, or pets. Encourage parents to donate a book for their child's birthday. If you ask others to donate books, also provide a list of suggested high-quality, appropriate books.

• *Remember that it takes time to create a great classroom library.* A library can't be created in a few weeks. Once you start the process, put your energy into enhancing the library and its surrounding area. Keep books looking nice, and place category labels on shelves to make it easier for students to find books. Use beanbag chairs and throw rugs to make the classroom library a comfortable place to hang out.

(Text continued on page 114)

Figure 5.3   Student Interest Inventory

Name: _____

1. What are your favorite hobbies?

2. What are your favorite television shows?

3. What is your favorite place to eat out?

4. What is your favorite book and why do you like it so much?

5. Who read to you when you were younger? Explain.

6. Do you have a library card for the public library?

7. How often do you visit the school or public library?

8. Approximately how many books do you read each year?

9. What parts of reading do you like the most and the least?

Figure 5.4   Reading Inventory

Name: _____

1. Do you like to read? Circle: Yes or No. Why or why not?

2. How often do you read on your own?

3. How many books have you read in the past 6 months? How many of those books did you choose to read?

4. What do you look for when you choose a book to read?

5. Where do you find the books you read? Circle as many as apply.

   Home

   Friends

   Bookstore

   Classroom

   School library

   Public library

   Other (describe): _____

6. List some of your favorite writers or describe the kinds of books you like to read.

7. Do you consider yourself a good reader? Why or why not?

- *Conduct before- or afterschool sessions.* Some students benefit greatly from coming to school a little early or staying after classes to work on their reading skills in small groups. Consider this time a "triple dip," or a third time each day that students receive intensive reading instruction.

- *Carefully select texts.* Sequence books to ensure student success. Choose books at the students' independent or instructional level.

- *Organize learning activities.* Use structured learning activities during intervention sessions. Activities might include reading the text together and working on comprehension strategies, concentrating on letter sounds, or building background knowledge.

- *Create small intervention groups.* Keep intervention groups small (three to eight students) to ensure that you have time to work with each student individually. Meet with the group daily or several times each week. Be sure to give an assignment to the rest of the students so that they will not distract the intervention group's work. Give the intervention group a sense of privacy by allowing the group to work at a table set aside in one corner of the room.

- *Use fast-paced instruction.* Many teachers slow down their instructional pace when working with struggling students. By slowing the pace, teachers doom students to staying behind perpetually. Instead of slowing the pace, develop a sense of urgency when working with struggling students.

◼ READING ALOUD TO STUDENTS

Another important component of a well-balanced literacy program is reading aloud to students. When teachers read books aloud to their students, they provide students with an opportunity to learn about unfamiliar books and genres, and they help students learn to visualize stories in their heads. In addition, reading aloud increases students' listening comprehension, an important skill for all students in a classroom setting.

Every time you read aloud to students, you model good reading skills. It is important for students to hear good reading techniques—from fluency to voice inflection—so they can imitate these techniques in their own reading. In addition, reading aloud to students increases their vocabulary and background knowledge, two critical components to developing strong reading comprehension.

How to Recognize a Good Read-Aloud Book

There are many, many good books to read aloud to your students. Remember to select books that you are excited and passionate about. Choose a book with the following characteristics to read aloud to students:

- The universal plot relates to students' lives and speaks to them.
- The plot pulls listeners into the story and keeps them involved, entertained, and interested.
- The characters are unforgettable, unique, and believable and are worth knowing and caring about.
- The setting allows students to experience a new and different environment.

- The story has the power to expand students' personal lifetime experiences.
- The language flows well when read aloud.
- The language is playful, fun, and enticing.
- The story makes students feel something (happy, sad, etc.).
- The ending is logical, satisfying, or surprising.
- The story broadens children's literary knowledge and experiences and leads them to similar books.
- The story does not use stereotypes or clichés.
- The story includes interesting discussions that allow students to reevaluate their opinions or prejudices.
- The illustrations are dynamic and strengthen and extend the story.
- The story spawns meaningful writing activities.
- Other teachers or readers recommend the book.

Brain Bits

Research has proven that the brain needs *active participation* in order to process information and make meaning of it. When teaching reading, it is one thing to tell students how to process information and a whole other thing to ask them to use what they have learned in a meaningful way. As David Sousa explained in *How the Brain Learns*, Third edition (2006), practice does not make perfect; it makes *permanent* (p. 97). The purpose of actively practicing a newly learned skill is to help the learner use this skill in a new situation with accuracy so that it will be remembered correctly and stored. Sousa recommends that before a student begins to practice, though, the teacher should model the thinking process involved in the skill and guide the student through each step in applying the learning.

Reciprocal teaching (Palincsar & Brown, 1984) is a strategy that applies this brain research to reading instruction. Reciprocal teaching promotes a dialogue between teachers and students regarding parts of text. The dialogue encompasses four activities: summarizing, generating questions, clarifying, and predicting. The teacher and students take turns assuming the role of teacher in leading the dialogue. The purpose of reciprocal teaching is to facilitate a group effort between teacher and students as well as among students in the task of bringing meaning to the text. The most important part of reciprocal teaching is that it actively involves students in making meaning out of what they are reading. Program evaluations have shown that this technique has been very successful in increasing students' reading skills.

ENCOURAGING PARENTS TO PARTICIPATE IN THEIR CHILD'S READING

Parents are a child's first and most important teacher, and it is critical that you encourage them to support their child's reading habits. Some parents do it naturally while others can benefit from a few suggestions from their child's teacher. Distribute the list of Ten Things Parents Can Do to Help Their Children Become Better Readers (Figure 5.7) to parents at a back-to-school night, with student report cards, or at parent conferences.

Tips for Reading Aloud

➤ Choose a book that you enjoy and believe your students will enjoy.

➤ Know why you are reading the book to students. You may choose a book to introduce students to a certain author, motivate students to read more, or expose them to a specific subject or topic. Be sure your reading-aloud plan includes discussion and questions that will encourage students to think about and analyze the reading.

➤ Preview the text, decide how you will deal with difficult situations, and think of questions you can ask your students about the story or characters.

➤ Practice reading the book or selection aloud before actually reading it to the class.

➤ Introduce the book and talk to students about the author, the subject matter, and any other background information they may need to know before you read the text. Use this introduction time to gain the interest of your students.

➤ Involve your students by showing them the book cover and asking them to predict what will happen in the story.

➤ Make sure students are seated comfortably and away from distraction. Start reading only when you have everyone's attention.

➤ Make eye contact with your students as you read (if possible).

➤ Try to stop at a natural point, such as the end of a chapter or at a cliffhanger moment.

➤ Take time after you read to discuss the story and characters and ask questions that will help students reflect on what they heard.

■ ASSESSING READING COMPREHENSION

One of the few ways you can confidently assess your students' comprehension is asking them to share their thoughts with you. Students' responses to what they are reading give you windows into their minds. This is not to say that standardized tests aren't valuable assessments. Standardized tests allow you to view how individual students are doing compared with their peers. However, it is critical to know what is going on inside a student's head—the process he or she follows—when reading. Standardized tests simply cannot capture this step-by-step reading process, but informal techniques can. You can build informal assessments of students into your classroom routine. Following are some ideas from Harvey and Goudvis (2000) for informally assessing students' reading comprehension:

- *Listen to students.* Listen to what students say after they read a text.

- *Listen in on students' conversations.* Eavesdropping on students' conversations with one another about what they are reading allows you to ascertain what they are thinking about and how they are processing the text.

- *Observe expressions and body language.* Watch students carefully and notice their expressions while they read. Expressions and body language give you a glimpse into what students are thinking and feeling. A puzzled look or a scrunched up nose tells you a lot.

- *Chart responses and conversations in group discussions.* Record what students say in class discussions on a chart, and encourage students to refer to the chart.

- *Hold conferences with students.* Meet one-on-one with students to help them sort out their thinking and processing.

- *Keep anecdotal records of conferences and conversations.* Take notes after talking to a student or hearing a conversation. You may collect the notes in a three-ring notebook that has a divider for each student. Simply jot down a note or two when it is convenient to help create a running record of students' thinking.

- *Examine and evaluate student writing samples.* Use students' written responses to discern whether students are making meaning out of what they are reading.

Figure 5.7   Ten Things Parents Can Do to Help Their Children Become Better Readers

1. *Read to your child.* Try to read to your child every day. Read from a wide variety of materials and books.

2. *Encourage your child to write.* Encourage young children to scribble and pretend to write. Encourage older children to write stories and letters and share them with the family. Make sure writing materials are readily available.

3. *Provide reading material at home.* Be sure that many and various books, children's magazines, and newspapers are available for children to look at and read.

4. *Obtain a library card for your child and take your child to the library and to bookstores.* Go to the public library or local bookstore frequently. Take time to look at different books and check out new books.

5. *Control the television.* Turn off the television and provide quiet time for reading. Watch shows that help your child learn about specific subjects. This will increase your child's background knowledge and will help your child when he or she reads about those subjects.

6. *Engage in conversation.* Talk to your child often about a wide variety of subjects. Talk about family issues, the world, animals, hobbies, and your child's reading.

7. *Value school and learning.* Visit your child's class and show interest in your child's stories about school. Praise your child's academic achievement.

8. *Do many informal educational activities.* Visit zoos, museums, and different places. Challenge your child to cook, draw, and paint. Try to offer your child a wide range of opportunities and experiences.

9. *Ask your child to read aloud.* Encourage your child to read aloud to you and other family members. Help your child overcome mistakes. If the book seems too difficult, find an easier one. A good test is the five-finger rule. If your child stumbles over five or more words on a single page, then the book is too difficult.

10. *Model reading.* Take time to read and let your child see you reading.

■ A LAST LOOK AT THE TEACHER AS A PROMOTER OF LITERACY

Becoming a good literacy teacher is a lifelong pursuit. Literacy holds the key to students' future success. Therefore, it is essential for students to master literacy. The sooner students learn to read, the sooner they begin to read to learn. Ensure that your students have the head start they need in life; endeavor to become increasingly skilled in teaching literacy and creating a classroom environment that promotes reading and writing. Whether you teach elementary, middle, or high school, strive to be the best literacy teacher you can be.

■ RECOMMENDED READINGS

Allington, R. (2001). *What really matters for struggling readers: Designing research-based programs.* New York: Longman.

Gallagher, K. (2003). *Reading reasons: Motivational mini-lessons for middle and high school.* Portland, ME: Stenhouse.

Robb, L. (2000). *Teaching reading in middle school: A strategic approach to teaching reading that improves comprehension and thinking.* New York: Scholastic.

Figure 5.8 Glossary of Reading Terms

This glossary contains terms that are commonly used when reading or talking about reading. Most of these terms have been discussed in this chapter; a few more have been added to help you become familiar with terms that you might hear as you learn more about reading instruction.

Automaticity Readers' automatic recognition of words, a critical step in unlocking meaning for proficient readers.

Concepts of print Insights about how print works in English. Basic concepts about print include understanding that print comes in many forms, recognizing that print corresponds to speech, understanding how stories work, developing concepts about spacing and words, knowing the difference between letters and words, understanding parts of a book, and learning that print has directionality (text moves from left to right, top to bottom, front to back).

Decodable texts Reading materials that provide an intermediate step between learning words in isolation and reading authentic literature. Such texts are designed to give students an opportunity to learn to use their understanding of phonics in reading text.

Decoding A series of strategies used selectively by readers to recognize and read written words. Within a word, the reader locates cues (e.g., letter-sound correspondences) that reveal enough about the word to help in pronouncing it and attaching meaning to it.

Explicit instruction The intentional design and delivery of information by the teacher to the students. First the teacher models a skill or strategy; then the students practice and apply the skill or strategy in a structured exercise under the direction and guidance of the teacher; and finally, the students receive feedback from the teacher.

Expository text A traditional form of written composition. The primary purpose of expository text is to explain details, facts, and discipline- or content-specific information.

Fluency The ability to express ideas easily and quickly in written or spoken form; freedom from word-identification problems that hinder comprehension in silent reading or the expression of ideas in oral reading.

Graphic organizer An organized, visual representation of facts and concepts gleaned from a text. Graphic organizers help teachers and students represent abstract information in a concrete form, depict the relationships among facts and concepts, organize and elaborate ideas, and relate new information to prior knowledge.

Listening comprehension The ability to understand and comprehend the meaning of what a speaker is saying.

Literary criticism The result of literary analysis; a judgment or evaluation of a work or a body of literature.

Morpheme A linguistic unit that cannot be divided into smaller meaningful parts; the smallest meaningful part of a word.

Narrative A story or narrated account of actual or fictional events.

Onset and rime Intersyllabic units that are smaller than words and syllables but larger than phonemes. The onset is the portion of the syllable that precedes the vowel. (For example, in the word *black,* the onset is *bl.*) The rime is the portion of the syllable, including vowels and consonants, that follows the onset. (For example, in the word *black,* the rime is *ack.*) Although not all syllables or words have an onset, they all have a rime. (For example, the syllable or word *out* is a rime that does not have an onset.)

Orthographic Pertains to orthography, the art or study of correct spelling according to established usage.

Orthography The art or study of correct spelling according to established usage.

Phonemes The smallest units of speech that distinguish one utterance or word from another in a given language (e.g., the /r/ in *rug* or the /b/ in *bug*).

(Continued)

Figure 5.8   (Continued)

Phonemic awareness The understanding that every spoken word is made up of a sequence of phonemes or speech sounds. This awareness is essential for learning to read an alphabetic language because phonemes are represented by letters. Without phonemic awareness, phonics makes no sense; consequently, the spelling of words can be learned only by rote.

Phonemic awareness instruction Teaching awareness of words, syllables, and phonemes along a developmental continuum that includes rhyming substitution. Early phonemic instruction should focus on exploring the auditory structure of spoken language, not on letter-sound correspondences.

Phonics A system of teaching reading and spelling that stresses basic symbol-sound relationships and their application in decoding words. Phonics includes instruction in how to recognize, produce, isolate, blend, segment, and manipulate phonemes.

Predictable text Reading material that supports the prediction of certain features of text. Text is predictable when it enables students to predict quickly and easily what the author is going to say and how the author is going to say it on the basis of their knowledge of the world and of language.

Reading comprehension The ability to apprehend meaning from print and understand text. At a literal level, comprehension is the understanding of what an author has written or the specific details provided in a text. At a higher level, comprehension involves reflective and purposeful understanding that is thought-intensive, analytic, and interpretive.

Retelling The paraphrasing of a story in a student's own words; used to check the student's comprehension of the text. Sometimes, retelling is followed by questions that elicit further information.

Scaffolding The temporary support, guidance, or assistance provided to a student for a new or complex task. For example, students work in partnerships with a more advanced peer or adult who scaffolds the task by engaging in appropriate instructional interactions designed to model, assist, or provide necessary information. The interactions should eventually lead to independence.

Schema A reader's organized knowledge of the world that provides a basis for comprehending, learning, and remembering ideas in stories and texts.

Sentence types

Declarative. A sentence that makes a statement.

Exclamatory. A sentence that makes a vehement statement or conveys strong or sudden emotion.

Imperative. A sentence that expresses a command, direction, or request.

Interrogative. A sentence that poses a question or makes an inquiry.

Sight words (or sight vocabulary) Words that the reader reads automatically, because they are familiar to the reader.

Spelling The forming of specific words by placing letters in the correct order according to established usage; orthography.

Word attack (or word analysis) A process used to decode words. Students are taught multiple strategies to identify a word. These strategies progress from decoding individual letter-sound correspondences, recognizing letter combinations, applying phonics analysis and rules, and using syllabication rules to analyze structural elements, including prefixes, suffixes, and roots.

Word recognition The identification and subsequent translation of the printed word into its corresponding sound and meaning.

Questions for Reflection

What types of instructional strategies can I use to strengthen my students' literacy skills?

_____

_____

_____

_____

How can I teach students to use and apply reading comprehension strategies?

_____

_____

_____

_____

How can I make my classroom library an exciting place for students to visit?

_____

_____

_____

_____

What type of professional reading might I do to become a better promoter of literacy?

_____

_____

_____

_____

Teacher as a Facilitator and Guide for Learning

"HOW DO I MANAGE AND ORGANIZE ACTIVITIES SO THAT MY STUDENTS LEARN?"

It is easy to think that as a teacher you must know all the information and answers. Most of us believe teachers should know it all because as children we believed our teachers knew it all. We were amused when we were able to stump our teachers. However, today's educational setting is different. Teachers can no longer have all the answers because information doubles every 12 months (if not faster) and the Internet disseminates information at ever faster rates. It is simply impossible for teachers to be the dispensers of all knowledge. The quicker you lose the notion that you should be the knowledge dispenser, the better a teacher you will be.

> The quicker you lose the notion that you should be the knowledge dispenser, the better teacher you will be.

One of the most important things you can do as a teacher is to empower your students to take in knowledge and information and make it their own. Students need to know how to learn, not just what to learn. You can teach students how to learn by facilitating their learning rather than by instructing students directly. It is important to realize that there is a time and a place for direct instruction. Many skills, strategies, and other bits of information must be directly and systematically taught to students. Yet at other times, it is more appropriate to allow students to experience learning for themselves. They need to discover ideas, practice newly learned skills, and review information on their own terms. When students interact with information through classroom activities, their motivation to learn, their memory of what they learned, and their desire to know more increase greatly.

To provide these types of learning opportunities, you must add facilitation strategies to your teacher's toolbox. Facilitating learning simply means organizing activities in which students can actively explore learning by themselves or with other students. To assure that all students can accomplish their goals, a good facilitator pays attention to how students work together. The facilitator challenges students' thinking, asks probing questions, and summarizes the group's issues. A strong facilitator provides clear directions, recognizes when students are floundering, and helps students get back on track. As students work in groups or independently, the facilitator monitors students' understanding and challenges them to think more deeply about specific subjects.

A teacher can facilitate learning in a classroom in many different ways; it's impossible to capture them all in a single chapter. In fact, you have already learned numerous approaches and teaching strategies, and you will learn more throughout your career. This chapter focuses on the most powerful strategies you can use to facilitate learning with your students. The strategies include cooperative learning, effective questioning, learning centers, graphic organizers, meaningful homework, and cross-age tutoring.

■ COOPERATIVE LEARNING

Students may interact with one another in three ways. They may interact *competitively*, comparing their own work with others' to see whose is best.

They may work *individually*, learning alone without paying attention to other students. And they may interact *cooperatively*, learning within a group and taking an interest in one another's learning as well as their own.

While it would seem that all three types of interaction would be common within a classroom, research shows that a vast majority of American students view school as a competition to outdo other students (Johnson & Johnson, 1999). While competition is appropriate at certain times and in certain places, society often calls for people to work cooperatively to achieve success. Now more than ever, students need to learn how to work with others in a positive and productive way. Businesses of the twenty-first century seek individuals who are skillful and knowledgeable and who also know how to work as a valuable member of a team.

> **Students need to learn how to work with others in a positive and productive way.**

Cooperative group work requires more than just placing students in groups. Cooperative groups must include the elements of cooperative learning defined by Johnson and Johnson (1999):

1. *Positive Interdependence.* Group members share a sense that they sink or swim together.

2. *Face-to-Face Promotive Interaction.* Group members help one another learn. The group recognizes the success and effort of each group member.

3. *Individual and Group Accountability.* Each member contributes to the group in a quest to achieve the goal.

4. *Interpersonal and Small-Group Skills.* Students are taught the skills they need to be positive members of a group. The skills include communication, trust, leadership, decision making, and conflict resolution.

5. *Group Processing.* Students are given time to reflect on how well the team functions and how to improve.

Getting Started With Cooperative Learning Groups

It is one thing to know how important cooperative learning is and another to use cooperative learning groups in your classroom. Cooperative learning takes practice and patience. Use these tips to organize groups and use cooperative learning in your classroom:

- Use a variety of criteria to group students. You can use criteria such as interests, birth dates, clothing characteristics, random drawings, or first letters of students' names. Use ability grouping infrequently and only for specific purposes.
- Choose different types of groups for different projects.

  Use informal groups for processing information, closure activities, and quick discussions.

  Use formal groups for completing assignments that last for several days or weeks.

Use base groups to provide students with support throughout the year in various activities. You may choose to have base groups sit together or to assign students to base groups for specific activities such as physical education games or art.

- Keep groups small (three to five students).
- Avoid overusing cooperative learning. Like any classroom method, cooperative learning can be overused. Remember, variety is important in creating and maintaining an interesting and effective classroom.

First Week Flag

Getting to Know One Another

Two of your goals during the first week of school are encouraging students to get to know one another and acquainting yourself with your students. Use cooperative learning to accomplish these goals. Group students randomly and ask them to complete assignments together. The assignment is not as important as the opportunity for cooperative learning. Some sample cooperative learning activities include making group posters for each of the classroom rules or building something using a few pieces of paper, paper clips, glue, and other materials. As students work in their groups, encourage them to talk and share. Take time to join each group to observe and talk with students.

■ EFFECTIVE QUESTIONING

Asking questions is a powerful strategy for facilitating learning. The quicker you realize that you don't need to provide students with all the information and answers, the quicker students take responsibility for their learning. Through the effective, regular use of questioning, you will help students learn to find answers for themselves as well as to think critically about specific subjects.

> **Asking questions is a powerful strategy for facilitating learning.**

Take time to learn to be a thoughtful questioner. One of the mistakes teachers make is to ask questions about unusual rather than important ideas. Make sure you know what you want students to learn and understand, then target your questions toward those ideas. Sometimes the most unusual and exciting facts will be the most important, and at other times, these facts will not be important.

Socratic Questioning: Beyond Yes or No

Socratic questioning is a powerful teaching strategy for fostering critical thinking. You can model intellectual curiosity by continually asking probing questions. Begin the discussion by posing questions that foster evaluation, promote critical thinking, encourage students to consider different perspectives, and challenge students to apply knowledge about the subject. Follow up student answers with more questions that help students think in a disciplined, intellectually responsible manner. When you use Socratic questioning, be sure to do the following:

- Keep the discussion focused. (It can easily get off track.)
- Guide students to dig deeper, giving complex rather than simple answers to complex questions.
- Stimulate the discussion with probing questions. (See the sidebar titled "Probing Questions" on page 130 for examples.)
- Periodically summarize what students have or have not discussed or resolved.
- Draw as many students as possible into the discussion.

Becoming proficient at using Socratic questioning takes time and practice. Here are some bits of advice to help along the way:

- *Establish norms (rules) for answering questions.* Norms may include raising a hand before speaking, being respectful listeners, not interrupting others, and valuing one another's opinions. Remind students of these norms frequently and post them so students can refer to them on a regular basis.

- *Avoid yes-no questions.* Rather than asking students, "Do you understand?" try saying, "Give me an example so I know you understand."

- *Make sure students have enough background knowledge and know enough information to respond to the questions.* If students don't know very much about a topic, they will not be able to reflect deeply on that topic.

- *Use questions from all levels of thinking to help develop students' comprehension and higher-order thinking skills.* Bloom's taxonomy defines many different levels of questioning. (See the next section and Table 6.1.)

- *Allow sufficient wait time after posing a question.* Some students need more time to process information than others. (See the sidebar titled "Wait Time" on page 130 for more information.)

- Give other active learning opportunities for students to respond to questions (e.g., think-pair-share and journal writing).

Bloom's Taxonomy: Levels of Questioning

Bloom (1956) created a taxonomy of the levels of questions that commonly occur in classrooms (see Table 6.1). The taxonomy provides a useful structure in which to categorize questions. Most teachers characteristically ask questions within a particular level. To overcome this habit, take time to learn the levels and ask questions from a variety of levels.

Classroom Approaches to Facilitate Student Questioning

Effective questioning can be embedded across the curriculum to support your students' investigations, discussions, and explorations of information. You may choose from several different approaches that boost student learning through strategic questioning. The goal is to get students

Probing Questions

➤ What do you mean by _____?

➤ What is your main point?

➤ How does _____ relate to _____?

➤ Could you state that another way?

➤ What do you think is the main issue here?

➤ Can you give an example?

➤ Why do you say that?

➤ What are you assuming when you give that answer?

➤ How do you justify that assumption?

➤ Why do you think that is right?

➤ How does this apply to your case?

➤ Could you explain your reasons to us?

➤ What would someone who disagrees say?

➤ What is an alternative?

➤ But if that happened, what else would happen as a result?

➤ What are the important points of the article?

➤ Is this question easy or hard to answer, and why?

Wait Time

Rowe (1972) invented the concept of wait time as an instructional tool. She conducted research in the classroom to determine how long teachers typically waited for students to respond to questions. She found that the wait time between the teacher's question and the students' answers rarely lasted more than 1.5 seconds. She also discovered that when the wait time was increased to 3 seconds, these positive outcomes occurred:

➤ The length and correctness of students' responses increased.

➤ The number of "I don't know" responses decreased.

➤ The number of voluntary, appropriate answers greatly increased, as did the numbers of students giving answers.

➤ Students' scores on academic achievement tests tended to increase.

➤ Teachers' questioning strategies tended to be more varied and flexible.

➤ Teachers decreased the quantity and increased the quality and variety of questions.

➤ Teachers asked additional questions that required students to use more complex processing and higher-order thinking.

thinking critically about what they are learning, responding to questions orally and in written form, and being accountable for what they read and study. Following are some questioning techniques that help students think critically about what they are learning:

• *Questioning the Author.* Encourage students to assume greater responsibility for their learning by actively interacting with text and engaging in discussions about the meaning of text. Teach students how to ask questions of the author, such as, why did this author choose the point of view of the child instead of the father? or what type of childhood did the author have that may have made him or her interested in these things?

• *Thin and Fat Questions.* Explain the difference between thin (literal) and fat (higher-order) questions to students. "What happened in the story?" is a thin question because it asks students to merely give back information without doing much critical thinking. On the other hand, how do you feel the Civil War was different from and similar to the

Table 6.1   Bloom's Taxonomy

Cognitive Level	Some of the Things Students Demonstrate When They Are Working at This Level	Activities
Knowledge	• Recall information. • Know dates, events, places. • Understand major ideas. • Master subject matter.	List, define, tell, describe, identify, show, label, collect, examine, tabulate, quote, name (who, when, where, etc.)
Comprehension	• Understand information. • Grasp meaning. • Translate knowledge into new context. • Interpret, compare, and contrast facts. • Order, group, and infer causes. • Predict consequences.	Summarize, describe, interpret, contrast, predict, associate, distinguish, estimate, differentiate, discuss, extend
Application	• Use information. • Use methods, concepts, and theories in new situations. • Solve problems using required skills or knowledge.	Apply, demonstrate, calculate, complete, illustrate, show, solve, examine, modify, relate, change, classify, experiment, discover
Analysis	• Recognize patterns. • Organize parts. • Recognize hidden meanings. • Identify components.	Analyze, separate, order, explain, connect, classify, arrange, divide, compare, select, explain, infer
Synthesis	• Use old ideas to create new ones. • Generalize from given facts. • Relate knowledge from several areas. • Predict outcomes and draw conclusions.	Combine, integrate, modify, rearrange, substitute, plan, create, design, invent, compose, formulate, prepare, rewrite
Evaluation	• Compare and discriminate between ideas. • Assess value of theories and presentations. • Make choices based on reasoned argument. • Verify value of evidence. • Recognize subjectivity.	Assess, decide, rank, grade, test, measure, recommend, convince, select, judge, explain, discriminate, support, conclude, compare, summarize

SOURCE: From Benjamin S. Bloom et al., *Taxonomy of Educational Objectives.* Published by Allyn and Bacon, Boston, MA. Copyright © 1984 by Pearson Education. Adapted by permission of the publisher.

Revolutionary War? is a fat question because it requires students to evaluate and synthesize information. Take time to ask students to identify the different types of questions as you ask them.

• *Chalk Talk.* During this silent activity, students reflect on a question and write ideas sparked by the question. Begin by writing the driving question (e.g., in what ways are socialism and communism similar?) in the center of a large piece of butcher paper. Allow each student to silently respond to the question by writing on the paper. Explain that students can respond to others' responses by expanding, commenting, circling, or connecting interesting ideas together. It usually takes a little while to warm up to this type of activity, so it's important to allow enough time for students to respond.

• *Questioning the Reader.* Assign a student to ask questions of other students after a short silent-reading passage. You can also ask students to take turns asking questions of one another in small groups.

Reading Comprehension Questions

A common questioning activity is asking questions after students read a text. Be sure to choose questions that focus on the targeted goal for student reading.

Worthwhile Web Sites

The following sites offer resources for facilitating learning:

A to Z Teacher Stuff (www.atozteacherstuff.com)

Awesome Library (www.awesomelibrary.org)

Frank and Mike's Physical Education Page
(www.geocities.com/sissio/physical_education.html)

Homework Online (www.homework-online.com)

Intel Innovation in Education—Teaching With Technology (www.intel.com/education)

Jigsaw Center (www.jigsaw.org)

• *Right There Questions.* If you want students to read for literal comprehension, ask *right there* questions. Students can find the answers to these questions easily within the text without much effort.

• *Think and Search Questions.* If you want students to draw conclusions from several parts of the text, ask *think and search* questions. Students must find information in several parts of the text in order to answer these questions.

• *In My Head Questions.* If you want students to answer from their own background knowledge and experiences, ask *in my head* questions. Students must find the answers to these questions within their own background knowledge and experiences rather than in the text.

■ LEARNING CENTERS

Remember to tie all learning centers to your curriculum, standards, and learning goals.

In classroom learning centers, students work, alone or in small groups, on specific projects or assignments. Learning centers allow students opportunities to learn actively and to internalize knowledge about a subject. There is no "right" way to create or manage centers. However, you must remember to tie all learning centers to your curriculum, standards, and learning goals. As long as you make those connections and ensure that centers are not just busy work, your learning centers will be a great asset to your classroom. How many centers you operate at one time depends on the size of your classroom and potential learning center space, the number of parents available to help, and your curriculum plans.

Understanding Types of Centers

Learning centers fall into three categories: curriculum-based, thematic, and can't-get-to-it-any-other-way.

• *Curriculum-based learning centers* relate directly to the material you are teaching. They allow students to review and work with the material on their own. For example, if your class is studying ancient Egypt in social studies, you might create a curriculum-based learning center that includes books and computer resources about Egyptian pyramids. You might ask students to research pyramids, design their own pyramids, and write a one-page explanation of the importance and relevance of pyramids in ancient Egypt. Finally, you might conclude the activity by asking students to hypothesize reasons Egypt was one of only a few ancient civilizations to build and use pyramids.

• *Thematic learning centers* focus on a theme you are teaching. For example, students might be reading about the California gold rush in their reading time and also studying this period in social studies. You might create a thematic learning center in which students write a short play about the gold rush days, including pertinent places and other information. You might create another center in which students study old maps and draw their own maps detailing the major gold rush towns and areas.

• *Can't-get-to-it-any-other-way learning centers* can help relieve your guilt when you simply do not have time to include certain learning experiences during regular classroom time. For example, many upper-grade teachers complain that with the academic pressure turned up so high, they no longer have time for art, music appreciation, handwriting practice, and similar types of activities. These teachers can design centers that provide students opportunities to work in these areas after they complete their regular assignments. Instead of meandering around the room and being bored after completing an assignment, students can head to the music center to listen to and compare and contrast three classical pieces of music, for example.

Managing Centers

After you create a learning center, it is critical to review the activity and your expectations for the center with your entire class. Many behavior problems can be avoided by ensuring that students know exactly what they should do in each center.

Post learning center rules (Figure 6.1) at each center to remind students of your expectations for their behavior. Don't hesitate to temporarily take away a student's privilege of participating in learning centers if the student has not followed the rules. You may be amazed at how quickly the student's behavior will turn around.

Scheduling Centers

Following are some scheduling options for your learning centers. Remember that there is no one right way to schedule centers. Keep trying different schedules until you find some that work for you and your students.

Figure 6.1   Learning Center Rules

1. Do your very best work at all times.

2. Don't disturb those around you.

3. If you have a question, ask students in your center before you ask an adult.

4. When you complete your work, find something quiet to do at the center or at your desk.

5. Use your quiet, inside voice at all times.

6. Remember that center time is a privilege.

Specific-Days Center Time

Set aside specific days of the week to allow students to participate in centers. For example, you may choose to use Tuesday and Friday afternoons for centers for the majority of the class while you work with certain small groups to help them catch up in reading or math.

Follow-Up Center Time

After you complete a lesson with the class, you can use centers to review and reinforce what students just learned. Set up a series of centers that relate to the subject and rotate students through the centers.

Random Center Time

Allow individual students to visit centers when they complete their work. Since these centers are more relaxed in organization than the regular classroom is, remind students about the learning center rules and emphasize that this time is a privilege. If students don't follow the rules, they will lose their ability to use the learning centers. Most students don't want to lose your trust and will take this time as a privilege and act accordingly. If a student

Tips for Designing Learning Centers

➤ Use famous people's names for each center. For example, the Walt Whitman Center can be your writing center, the Dr. Seuss Center can be your classroom library center, the Steve Jobs (Macintosh founder) Center can be your technology center, and the Rosa Parks Center can be your civil rights center. Naming centers for famous people helps students learn these people's names in a fun and interactive way.

➤ Give centers a sense of place and privacy. Build nooks into your room so that students feel they are getting away from others when they work in a learning center.

doesn't follow the rules, consistently apply the rules and take away the privilege of working in centers for a time. Taking away this privilege temporarily will not only teach that student but will also signal to all your students that you mean what you say and that you value learning center time.

GRAPHIC ORGANIZERS ■

Graphic organizers are visual representations that help learners process information by means of structures for ordering main ideas and relationships. Graphic organizers can be used in whole-class discussions, small-group meetings, and individual homework assignments. When students take information and mold it into a graphic organizer, they use the rehearsal and elaboration processes that help them transfer the information into long-term memory. Some of the most common graphic organizers are presented in Figure 6.2.

MEANINGFUL HOMEWORK ■

Homework can have a very positive impact on a student's learning and academic success. Homework is defined as out-of-class tasks assigned to students as an extension or elaboration of classroom work. Teachers use homework to provide additional learning time, strengthen study and organizational skills, and, in some respects, keep parents informed of their children's progress.

There are three types of homework:

- *Practice assignments* reinforce newly acquired skills. For example, students who have just learned a new method of solving a mathematical problem should be given sample problems to complete on their own.
- *Preparation assignments* help students prepare for activities that will occur in the classroom. Students may be required to do background research on a topic to be discussed later in class.
- *Extension assignments* parallel class work and are frequently long-term, continuing projects. Students must apply previous learning to complete these assignments. Some sample extension assignments are science fair projects and term papers.

In the past several years, some have argued against homework. Kralovec, author of *The End of Homework* (2001), emphasized the negative aspects of homework in her speech to the American Youth Policy Forum held on Capitol Hill in November 2000. According to her research, homework actually pushed young people out of school because students who didn't complete their homework would most likely fail a class or series of classes and then drop out of school. Kralovec also felt that homework could have a negative and disruptive effect on children, families, and communities. Instead of building positive child-family relationships, parents and children spend their time arguing over homework. Homework also depletes the time available for many other important elements in life, including meal time, relaxation, music lessons, sports, or hanging out with

(Text continued on page 138)

Figure 6.2   Graphic Organizers

Timelines

Timelines are straight lines that have designations for times or dates. Timelines are used to show a sequence of events.

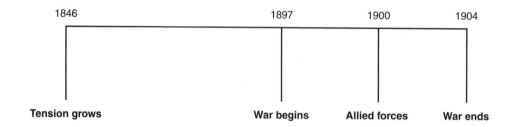

1846		1897	1900	1904
Tension grows		**War begins**	**Allied forces**	**War ends**

Diagrams

Diagrams come in many shapes and sizes. An example of a diagram is a comparison chart (like the one shown below).

Book 1	*Book 2*
Mystery genre	Science fiction genre
Two main characters	Five characters in book
Suspenseful	Conflict between father and
Solving crime	daughter drive the story
Ending is a big surprise	Ending is not surprising

Flowcharts

Flowcharts show a sequence of cause-and-effect events.

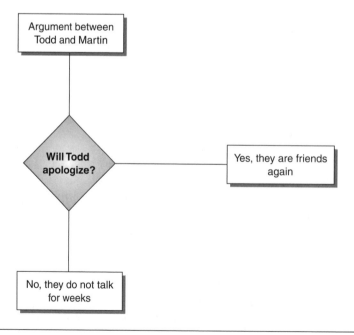

Outlines

Outlines organize data into a hierarchical pattern.

1. Main idea
    a. Supporting information
    b. Supporting information

2. Main idea
    a. Supporting information
    b. Supporting information

Venn Diagram

Venn diagrams use two overlapping circles to compare and contrast two objects or ideas. Students write the qualities that the objects or ideas do not share in the outside parts of the circle, and Write the qualities that the two objects or ideas do share in the overlapping section.

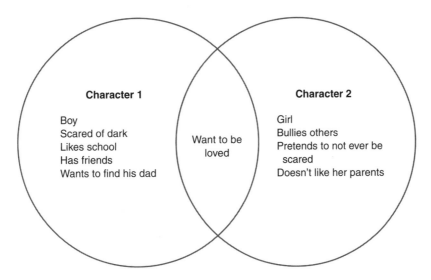

Character 1

Boy
Scared of dark
Likes school
Has friends
Wants to find his dad

Want to be loved

Character 2

Girl
Bullies others
Pretends to not ever be scared
Doesn't like her parents

Mind Maps

Mind maps can be used to help students identify a central idea in what they are studying and determine important and supporting ideas. Students write the central idea in the center of the map and link the other important and supporting ideas in a way that makes sense to the learner.

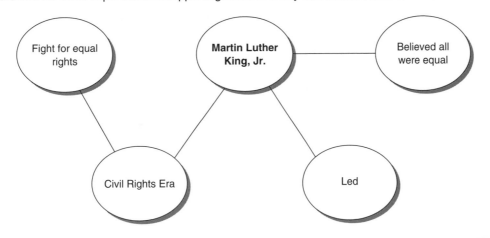

Fight for equal rights

Martin Luther King, Jr.

Believed all were equal

Civil Rights Era

Led

Brain Bits

The pace of life is hectic and leaves very little time for reflection. Yet reflection is critical for deep understanding. The brain needs time to think about what is being learned, to determine what is important, and to connect new and old information (Caine & Caine, 1991). Be sure to provide reflection time by asking students to think back on a lesson and reflect on what they are learning.

One technique to foster reflection is called *think-pair-share*. In this activity, you pose a question and then ask students to think silently for 2 minutes. Next, students pair off and share their thinking with their partner. Finally, students share their reflections with the whole class.

Another reflection technique is KWL (Ogle, 1986), described in Chapter 4. A KWL chart can be used at the beginning of a unit of study to activate students' background knowledge about a topic and focus their learning efforts as they identify what they already know and what they want to learn. If you used a KWL chart at the beginning of a unit, bring it out again at the end of the unit and ask students to think about how to fill in the last column of the chart, which asks them to identify what they have learned.

What Do We KNOW About _____?	*What Do We WANT to Know About _____?*	*What Have We LEARNED About _____?*

Remember that just as your students need reflection time, you also need time to think back on your teaching in order to identify where to make adjustments and changes. Build reflection into your busy schedule. Take time to write in a reflection journal or simply think about a lesson as you drive home in the afternoon. The more you reflect on your practice, the stronger a teacher you will become.

(Text continued from page 135)

friends. Kralovec also added that homework can punish poor children most of all because they generally lack parental structure and support as well as computer and Internet access.

Overall, homework has been shown to be beneficial to the learning process. However, it is important that you, as a teacher, recognize the arguments against assigning an overwhelming amount of homework. (See the sidebar on page 139 titled "How Much Homework Should I Give?" for further discussion.)

Five Strategies to Improve Homework Results

The following strategies will help your students experience greater success in their homework efforts. These strategies will also make it easier for you to achieve your goals of assigning specific homework activities to help in the learning process.

Strategy 1: Give Clear and Appropriate Assignments

Teachers need to take special care when assigning homework. If a homework assignment is too hard, is perceived as busy work, or takes too long to complete, students might tune out and resist doing it. Do not send home any assignment that students cannot do. Homework should be an extension of what students have learned in class. To ensure that homework is clear and appropriate, consider some of the following ideas:

- Make sure students and parents have information regarding the policies on missed and late assignments, extra credit, and available adaptations.
- Establish a routine at the beginning of the year for the way homework will be assigned.
- Assign work that the students can do.
- Assign homework in small units.
- Explain the assignment clearly.
- Write the assignment on the chalkboard and leave it there until the assignment is due.
- Remind students of when their homework is due.
- Coordinate with other teachers to prevent homework overload.
- Assign homework toward the beginning of class.
- Relate homework to class work or real life. (Tell students how they will use the content of the homework in real life.)
- Ask students to begin the homework in class, check that they understand, and provide assistance as necessary.
- Allow students to work together on homework.

Strategy 2: Make Homework Accommodations and Modifications

Make any necessary modifications to the homework assignment before sending it home. Identify practices that will be most helpful to individual students and that have the potential to increase their involvement, understanding, and motivation to learn. The most common homework accommodations include the following:

How Much Homework Should I Give?

Balance is the key. Provide enough homework to strengthen student learning, but avoid assigning too much homework lest you completely turn students off to the learning process. So, how much homework is the right amount? Unfortunately, this is a question without a clear and decisive answer.

The National PTA (www.pta.org) recommends the following amounts of homework:

➢ *Grades K–2*: 10–20 minutes per day.

➢ *Grades 3–6*: 30–60 minutes per day.

➢ *Grades 7–12*: Varying amounts according to the type and number of subjects a student is taking. In general, college-bound students receive lengthier and more involved homework assignments than do students preparing to enter the workforce immediately after graduation.

The amount of homework you assign your students may vary slightly from year to year depending on your students as well as your curriculum. Your most important guideline is to be sure that you assign meaningful homework that will help your students learn what you are trying to teach them.

- Provide additional one-on-one assistance to students.
- Monitor students' homework closely.
- Allow alternative response formats (e.g., allow a student to audiotape an assignment rather than handwriting it).
- Adjust the length of the assignment.
- Provide a peer tutor or assign the student to a study group.
- Provide learning tools (e.g., calculators).
- Adjust evaluation standards.
- Give fewer assignments.

It is important to check out all accommodations with other teachers, students, and their families. If teachers, students, or families do not find homework accommodations palatable, they may not use them.

Increasing Student Accountability With Homework Planners

One teacher used a homework planner to increase communication with students' families and improve homework completion rates. Students developed their own homework calendars. Each page in the calendar reflected one week. There was a space for students to write their homework assignments and a column for parent-teacher notes. The cover was a heavy card stock that students decorated. Students were expected to take their homework planners home each day and return to class with them the next day.

In conjunction with the homework planner, students graphed their homework return and completion rates—another strategy that is linked to homework completion and improved performance on classroom assessments. The teacher built a reward system for returning homework and the planners. On a self-monitoring chart in their planners, students, using one of the following systems, recorded each time they completed and returned their homework assignment:

➢ Coloring the square for the day green if homework was completed and returned

➢ Coloring the square for the day red if homework was not done

➢ Coloring one-half of the square yellow and one-half of the square red if homework was late

Strategy 3: Teach Study Skills

Veteran teachers consistently report that homework problems seem to be exacerbated by deficient study skills. Many students, particularly students with disabilities, need instruction in study and organizational skills. Here is a list of organizational strategies basic to completing homework:

- Identify a location for doing homework that is free of distractions.
- Be sure all materials are available and organized.
- Allocate enough time to complete activities and keep on schedule.
- Take good notes.
- Develop a sequential plan for completing multitask assignments.
- Check assignments for accuracy and completion before turning them in.
- Know how to get help when it is needed.
- Turn in completed homework on time.

Teachers can enhance homework completion and accuracy by providing classroom instruction in organizational skills. They should talk with parents about how to support the application of organizational skills at home.

Strategy 4: Use a Homework Calendar or Scheduler

Many students often need additional organizational support. Just as adults use calendars, schedulers, lists, and other devices to self-monitor activities, students can benefit from these tools as well. Students can monitor their own homework using a planning calendar to keep track of homework assignments. Homework planners also can double as home-school communication tools if they include a space next to each assignment for messages between teachers and parents.

Strategy 5: Ensure Clear Home-School Communication

Homework accounts for one fifth of the time that successful students invest in academic tasks, yet students complete homework in environments over which teachers have no control. Therefore, teachers and parents must communicate clearly and effectively with one another about homework policies, required practices, mutual expectations, student performance on homework, homework completion difficulties, and other homework-related concerns. Teachers can improve communication with parents by doing the following:

> ## Worthwhile Web Sites
>
> Here are a few Web sites that can help with homework:
>
> **Homeworkspot.com** (www.homeworkspot.com)
>
> **Infoplease Homework Center** (www.infoplease.com/homework)
>
> **National PTA** (www.pta.org)
>
> **School Notes** (Allows teachers to post school information for parents and students to access any time; www.schoolnotes.com)

- Encourage students to keep assignment books.
- Provide a list of suggestions about ways parents might assist with homework. For example, ask parents to check with their children about homework on a daily basis.
- Provide parents with frequent written communication about homework (e.g., progress reports, notes, letters, and forms).
- Share information with other teachers regarding students' strengths, needs, and necessary accommodations.
- Be clear on your homework policy. Is late homework acceptable? Will it get only half credit if it is late? Work out these details early in the year and make sure that all students and parents understand your homework policy so there are no surprises.

CROSS-AGE TUTORING ■

In cross-age tutoring, an older student tutors a younger one during the school day. This process is very powerful for the older student (who must thoroughly understand the subject before teaching it) and the younger student (who sees the older student as a role model to be emulated). This relatively simple idea takes organization, forethought, and structure to be successful. Follow these tips to make cross-age tutoring successful:

1. *Match students.* Take time to match up students who share similar interests or personality traits. Randomly assigning pairs often leads to students' not connecting with one another, which hinders the learning process.

2. *Train older students.* Don't assume that a group of older students naturally knows how to work with younger students. The more structured training you provide to your older students, the more successful the tutoring session will be. Be sure the teacher of the older students explains how to work with younger students and provides tips and suggestions along the way.

3. *Review expectations and outcomes.* Be very clear about what students should be working on and what the younger students need to learn. For example, tell students that by the end of the tutoring session, students must read the story and the younger student must answer two or three questions (that you have provided the tutor).

4. *Schedule regular tutoring sessions.* It is best to schedule tutoring sessions regularly or semiregularly. If sessions are random and infrequent, students will have limited continuity in the relationship, and each tutoring session will be focused on getting acquainted instead of on learning.

■ A LAST LOOK AT THE TEACHER AS A FACILITATOR AND GUIDE FOR LEARNING

This chapter shared some techniques that teachers can use to facilitate learning and encourage their students to become actively involved in their own learning process. Strong facilitators provide a structure and clear vision of what they want students to learn and be able to do. Then they get out of the way and allow the students to become deeply involved in the learning activity. Facilitating learning is not easy. In fact, it can take even more preparation time than direct instruction can. Yet the benefits for students are plentiful. When you see your students' eyes light up when they discover something for themselves, you will know that the work of being a good teacher-facilitator is well worth it.

■ RECOMMENDED READINGS

Armstrong, T. (1994). *Multiple intelligences in the classroom.* Alexandria, VA: Association for Supervision and Curriculum Development.

Campbell, B., & Campbell, L. (1999). *Multiple intelligences and student achievement: Success stories from six schools.* Alexandria, VA: Association for Supervision and Curriculum Development.

Fogarty, R. (1997). *Problem-based learning and other curriculum models for the multiple intelligences classroom.* Thousand Oaks, CA: Corwin Press.

Marzano, R. J., Pickering, D., & Pollock, J. (2001). *Classroom instruction that works: Research-based strategies for increasing student achievement.* Alexandria, VA: Association for Supervision and Curriculum Development.

Questions for Reflection

Why is it important that a teacher be a strong facilitator of learning?

_____

_____

_____

_____

What are some strategies that I could begin using right away to help facilitate learning?

_____

_____

_____

_____

How will the homework I assign guide student learning and not just be busy work?

_____

_____

_____

_____

What facilitation strategies do I want to use in my classroom right now and why?

_____

_____

_____

_____

Teacher as a Relationship Builder

Strategies for Connecting With Students
- Involve All Students
- Connect Through Class Meetings
- Hold Classroom Celebrations
- Use the Hot Seat
- Initiate Personal Communication
- Connect With Individual Students

Energy Givers and Energy Takers
- Student Energy Bandits

Supporting Students in Crisis

Strategies for Connecting With Parents
- Welcome Parent Volunteers
- Make Positive Phone Calls Home
- Show Appreciation Through Notes and Awards

Take Care of Yourself
- Emotional Health: The Foundation of Effective Teaching
- Balanced Living: Sleep, Nutrition, and Exercise

A Last Look at the Teacher as a Relationship Builder

Recommended Readings

Questions for Reflection

"HOW DO I BUILD RELATIONSHIPS WITH MY STUDENTS AND THEIR PARENTS?"

One of the most important things a teacher can do is put effort and thought into connecting with students and parents. Many parts of teaching are exhausting and energy sapping. Connecting with students and their parents is one part of the job that can give you energy. It is the lifeblood of teaching. When you feel connected to your students and when you share a hearty laugh with a parent, you will have a sense of contentment and satisfaction that will whisper, "You chose the right profession."

■ STRATEGIES FOR CONNECTING WITH STUDENTS

Building effective relationships with your students is the most important thing you will ever do. It enhances teaching and learning, decreases behavior problems, and helps you feel connected to your students. Developing relationships with students is a two-way street; it is just as much about listening as it is about talking. In this age of school shootings and escalating violence, it is more important than ever to help students feel connected to school and cared for as human beings. You can incorporate several simple activities into your schedule to help build meaningful relationships: involve all students, connect through class meetings, hold classroom celebrations, use the hot seat, initiate personal communication, and connect with individual students. Each of these activities is described in the following paragraphs.

> In this age of school shootings and escalating violence, it is more important than ever to help students feel connected to school and cared for as human beings.

Involve All Students

Do whatever you can to involve all students in class activities and discussions. Make a special effort to engage those quiet souls sitting in your room or those middle-of-the-road students who just finish their work and go home. Try changing the seating arrangement to ensure that all students sit near the front of the room at some time. During class discussions, allow for wait time after you ask questions so that students who don't process ideas as quickly as other students have time to formulate an answer.

Pull names from a jar to ensure involvement of all students during a class discussion. This strategy gives all students the message that they need to be engaged in the learning activity because they could be called on to respond at any time. This strategy also helps you avoid the common trap of calling mainly on the outgoing students who always raise their hands to answer questions.

Encourage student-to-student collaboration through partner and cooperative group activities. Do what you can to make sure that quiet and reluctant students are given every opportunity to participate and feel valued in your classroom.

Brain Bits

Gardner proposed the theory of multiple intelligences in his book *Frames of Mind: The Theory of Multiple Intelligences* (1983). He concluded that intelligence is not one fixed trait that dominates all the skills and problem-solving abilities students possess. Gardner (1983, 1993b) recognized seven intelligences:

➤ *Visual/spatial intelligence* is demonstrated through activities and interests regarding images, graphics, drawings, sketches, maps, charts, doodles, pictures, spatial orientation, puzzles, designs, looks, visual appeal, mind's eye, imagination, visualization, dreams, nightmares, films, and videos.

➤ *Verbal/linguistic intelligence* is demonstrated through activities and interests regarding words, wordsmithing, speaking, writing, listening, reading, papers, essays, poems, plays, narratives, lyrics, spelling, grammar, foreign languages, memos, bulletins, newsletters, newspapers, e-mail, faxes, speeches, talks, dialogues, and debates.

➤ *Musical/rhythmic intelligence* is demonstrated through activities and interests regarding music, rhythm, beat, melody, tunes, pacing, timbre, singing, opera, symphony, choir, chorus, madrigals, rap, rock, rhythm and blues, jazz, classical, folk, and advertisement jingles.

➤ *Bodily/kinesthetic intelligence* is demonstrated through activities and interests regarding art, activity, action, hands-on experiments, trying, doing, performance, plays, drama, sports, assembling and disassembling, forming and re-forming, manipulating, touching, feeling, immersion, and participation.

➤ *Interpersonal/social intelligence* is demonstrated through activities and interests regarding interaction, communication, conversation, sharing, understanding, empathy, sympathy, reaching out, caring, talking, whispering, laughing, crying, shuddering, socializing, meeting, greeting, leading, following, gangs, clubs, charisma, crowds, gatherings, and twosomes.

➤ *Intrapersonal/introspective intelligence* is demonstrated through activities and interests regarding self, solitude, meditation, thinking, creating, brooding, reflecting, envisioning, journaling, self-assessment, goal setting, plotting, planning, dreaming, fiction, nonfiction, poetry, affirmations, lyrics, songs, screenplays, commentaries, introspection, and inspection.

➤ *Naturalist intelligence* is demonstrated through activities and interests regarding nature, natural environment, listening, watching, observing, classifying, categorizing, discerning patterns, appreciating, hiking, climbing, fishing, hunting, snorkeling, diving, photography, trees, leaves, animals, living things, flora, fauna, ecosystems, sky, grass, mountains, lakes, and rivers.

Intelligence can be demonstrated through specific talents, skills, and interests. We can nurture and strengthen these intelligences in our students for maximum learning and achievement. We can also use these intelligences to build relationships with our students and their parents.

It is important to recognize that every single person you meet has a unique set of intelligences, and the more you pay attention and learn about each person, the better you will connect with and relate to each one.

Connect Through Class Meetings

Host whole-class meetings when they seem appropriate. Instead of always making decisions for your class, allow the entire class to meet and decide on certain issues. For example, if your class is misbehaving at lunch, hold a class meeting to discuss what kind of behavior (without naming names) is hurting the class and what must be improved. You might also ask the class to decide what games to play in PE, how to keep the room neater, what read-aloud to do next, and how to support one another better. Students enjoy feeling included in these types of meaningful discussions. Class meetings provide students with an opportunity to talk about things that are important to them and to feel valued by you.

Hold Classroom Celebrations

Don't shy away from celebrating achievements as a whole group. Celebrations can be small and quick; they need not consume an afternoon or feature cake and punch. For example, if the lunch duty supervisor has written you a note telling you that your class has improved its lunchroom behavior, share the note with your students. Then plan a 10-minute celebration, to be held before dismissal the next day. For example, tell students that due to their improved behavior, the class is going to celebrate by turning on some music and having 10 minutes of free time. This strategy is simple and painless, yet it gives students an opportunity to know that you are paying attention to and recognizing the good things they do.

Use the Hot Seat

The hot seat is a wonderful activity that helps students connect with one another and with you. It can be a great sponge activity when you find you have a few minutes to fill. Choose a hot seat—your chair, a special stool, or a student chair placed in the front of the room. Select a student to come to the front of the classroom and sit on the hot seat. Ask the class to think for a minute about all the good things about this student and then encourage volunteers to share their thoughts out loud. Students raise their hands and say things such as, "Karen is very considerate" or "John always shares his food at lunch." Remind students that they aren't required to say anything, but if they have something positive to say about the student, they should feel free to share. This may be one of the few times some students hear anything good about themselves.

The Art of Complimenting

As the teacher, it is important that you model the art of complimenting. Before using the hot seat activity for the first time, discuss the concept of compliments and ask students to give examples. You can always begin the hot seat activity by stating things such as, "I like the way Carol always makes time to help her friends when they have a problem." Giving some examples helps students understand what you are looking for when you ask them to think of something nice about that student.

Initiate Personal Communication

Challenge students to journal about what is on their mind or about activities they are doing. Take time to write replies to students, making the journals interactive.

Write a note to a student expressing your appreciation for something the student did in class or with another student. Giving notes is a concrete way to reinforce students' actions. Send positive notes home to parents commending students for their excellent behavior, improved homework, or anything else deserving of accolades.

Pick up the phone and call parents just to tell them how well their child is doing in your class. By your doing this, your students become keenly aware that you are on their side and are looking for their good deeds.

Worthwhile Web Sites

The following Web sites will support you as you work with parents and students:

Everything ESL (English as a Second Language; www.everythingesl.net)

National PTA (www.pta.org)

ReadyWeb (Getting students ready for school; readyweb.crc.uiuc.edu)

Scholastic (www.scholastic.com)

University of Kansas, Center for Research on Learning (www.ku-crl.org)

Connect With Individual Students

Take time to talk with students on an individual basis to learn about their interests and hobbies. Invite four or five students at a time to eat lunch with you. During lunch, ask students questions about themselves.

Many teachers highlight one student each week or month and ask that student to bring in pictures of family, hobbies, vacations, and pets to share with classmates. Once students feel that you are interested in them as people, they will feel much more connected to you, and you will feel more connected to them.

ENERGY GIVERS AND ENERGY TAKERS ■

Tom had been an elementary school teacher for 12 years. He was slumped in a back seat during a workshop and seemed to be dozing through most of the presentation when Bill first noticed him. Feeling sorry for the guy, Bill struck up a conversation during break. After Tom acknowledged his obvious lack of enthusiasm for the workshop, he began sharing with Bill how tired his class made him this year.

"I have never had a class that has taken so much out of me," he said with a sigh. "I have Robert, who talks all the time; Marissa, who is constantly out of her seat and gossiping about everyone else; and as an added bonus, I have the school bully, Todd, in my class. That's just to name a few. It's like they take a straw out in the morning and suck all the energy and life out of me. By the time the door slams shut behind them in the afternoon, I only have enough energy left to crawl out to my car and go home. I don't mean to sound pathetic; it's just a rough year."

Bill said that he too had had such experiences. He shared his philosophy that sometimes it is simply the chemistry of the class, and other times a few students can make it a really long year. Both men agreed that teaching is not fun when it takes all your energy and leaves you living the rest of your life on reserves.

The lifeblood of teaching is energy. Without it, the profession is simply exhausting. Your energy is bolstered and weakened many times throughout each day, depending on your environment, the individuals with whom you interact, and the way you take care of yourself. It is important that you learn to protect your own energy source and understand what bolsters and what diminishes your energy.

> Learn to protect your own energy source and understand what bolsters and what diminishes your energy.

Teaching is also a socially intensive career. In other words, the "product" of teaching is young people. Instead of churning out computer chips or shirts, you mold individuals who must be ready to succeed in life. You spend your days surrounded by many personality types and must figure out how to work successfully with a wide range of individuals. When you contemplate the many personalities you must interact with each day, it is enough to make you dizzy. During most days, you interact with the principal, the office manager, the janitor, parents, colleagues, and students.

Many of these individuals give you energy. Just talking to them makes you laugh or feel warm. Other individuals are simply neutral; they neither give nor take away energy. They may affect only the periphery of your life. Then there are those people who seem to take a straw and suck away your energy, drop by painful drop.

Learn to recognize who gives you energy and who drains your energy. Use the energy givers to help provide the joy in teaching. Learn to deal effectively with the energy bandits—those who take your energy away. Energy bandits come in all sizes, student and adult. In a general sense, each student energy bandit has an adult counterpart. It is important to note that these individuals are not "bad" or "mean." They simply take others' energy without even knowing they are doing it. The more aware you are of this phenomenon, the more you can protect your energy, and the longer you will happily stay in this profession.

Student Energy Bandits

Recognizing student energy bandits takes time. Most look just like regular students. Only after getting to know them and working with them do you realize that every time they leave your room, you are a little more tired than when they came in. Table 7.1 describes some of the energy bandits that a teacher might find in the classroom and the best ways to handle them.

■ SUPPORTING STUDENTS IN CRISIS

One of the most difficult and challenging times a teacher may face is helping a student who is in crisis. A crisis can occur in a student's life when

- Parents decide to get divorced
- A death occurs in the family
- Social problems arise
- Moods and emotions take over

Table 7.1   Student Energy Bandits

Student Type	Traits of This Student	How to Positively Handle This Student
Bill the Blamer	• Consistently blames you or everyone else for his problems. • Seems to live in a world that creates havoc for him. • Goes to great lengths to convince you that another student has ruined his project or tattles on someone who is bothering him in the reading corner.	Ignore the antics of Bill the Blamer. (This is easier said than done, but it is crucial to do so.) He gets his energy from knowing that his blaming is causing havoc and getting others in trouble.
Connie the Complainer	• Likes to hear her own voice. • Constantly complains about what isn't working but never does anything about it. • Gets her energy from griping and complaining. • Usually finds other students who don't mind listening to her complaints and some that will even join her in the complaint factory.	Turn the tables. Ask Connie the Complainer to fix whatever she complains about. Suggest that she write a letter to someone to fix a problem. She will quickly learn that she must be careful what she complains about as it will usually mean more work for her.
David the Drainer	• Asks for guidance, support, information, advice, and whatever he needs to feel better in the moment. • Follows you around the room needing you to explain the assignment just one more time. • Wants you to read his report before he turns it in because it might be wrong. • Frequently gets picked on by others due to his weakness or perceived areas of weakness.	David the Drainer's lack of confidence is furthered only if you allow him to depend on you for everything. Give him tools to get his needs met elsewhere. (For example, tell him to ask at least two students for help before asking you.) Don't enable him to continue his dependence on adults.
Brett the Bully	• Reprimands and puts down other students. • Pokes fun at others and ignores personal boundaries. • Gains energy and confidence by putting others in their place, usually in front of those he is trying to impress. • Stalks the playground looking for weak prey and then unleashes verbal or physical threats. • Attempts to contain himself inside the classroom, yet the behaviors usually seep out one way or another, and you are pulled in to referee. • Makes you feel as if you have gone into police work instead of teaching.	Zero tolerance is the only way to deal with Brett the Bully. Other students need to know that you simply will not stand for bullying in your classroom. As soon as he puts down or makes fun of someone, discipline him. Brett the Bully needs to know that the punishment will be swift and strong.

(Continued)

Table 7.1   (Continued)

Student Type	Traits of This Student	How to Positively Handle This Student
Debbie the Discounter	• Discounts or challenges everything you and others say. • Needs to be right and finds fault with any conflicting positions. • Is exhausting to converse with, so some students and teachers simply ignore her.	Choose your battles carefully and ignore all others. When the subject for debate is critical to Debbie the Discounter's growth, choose this battle and win it. However, most of the time she simply wants to start a debate. Ignore these attempts and move on.
Ginny the Gossip	• Talks about others behind their backs and receives a lot of energy from relaying the latest scoop. • Tries to earn her way into or keep herself in the "cool" crowd. (Ginny is usually a female.) • Lies about others, tells stories, and generally wreaks chaos in your class and on the playground. (This form of bullying is much harder to recognize than Brett's, and it can be quite an energy drain for you.)	Deal with Ginny the Gossip in an open and forthright manner. By nature, she does not want to be caught or she would be seen as a "big mouth" who shouts out in front of everyone. Therefore, catching her in the act and calling her parents can have a long-lasting effect.
Ruth the Rule Follower	• Revels in rules. (This student is cousin to Bill the Blamer.) • Knows all the class rules, obeys them to the letter, and expects others to do the same. This is a good thing by and large. • Righteously points out when others are not following the rules and expects you to deal with the sinner immediately. • Is usually not well liked by her peers and is seen as a goody-goody.	Since rules are in her nature, acknowledge when Ruth the Rule Follower is doing a nice job following the rules. For the sake of balance, let her know that the sky won't fall if she doesn't follow a rule. When she becomes the police of the classroom rules, kindly remind her that you are the teacher and you will enforce the rules yourself.

Sometimes students hide their crises for some time, but an attentive teacher can usually pick up clues that students are going through a difficult time. Figure 7.1 highlights three approaches you can take if you suspect or know that a student is in crisis. Each of these approaches is described in the following paragraphs.

• *Explore the problem with the student.* Help the student identify and define the issue and express feelings and emotions related to the crisis. Sometimes just having someone to talk to goes a long way in helping a student overcome problems.

• *Generate and assess alternatives and solutions with the student.* Help students brainstorm possible ways to cope with the problem and with their emotions. Examine the likely outcome of these ideas and choices with the student.

- *Create an action plan with the student.* Help the student choose viable alternatives and coping behaviors and identify what the next steps might include. Sometimes the next step is to simply ride out the storm, while at other times the student needs to talk with someone or write a letter or do some type of activity.

If you feel that the nature of the student's problem warrants further action, be sure to check with your administrator to understand the appropriate policies and procedures regarding options.

Figure 7.1   Strategies for Working With Students in Crisis

- ❑ Explore the problem.
- ❑ Generate and assess alternatives and solutions.
- ❑ Create an action plan.

STRATEGIES FOR CONNECTING WITH PARENTS ■

Parents are your greatest allies throughout teaching. Parents may be heavily invested in all that happens in your classroom because these happenings affect their child. However, some parents may not be interested at all due to other circumstances in their lives. Yet regardless of parents' current level of involvement, connecting with them is crucial. In fact, teachers' attempts to connect with parents usually increase parental involvement in the long run. And the more involved and positive parents are, the better their children will do in your class. Following are a few strategies you can use to connect with parents throughout the year. They include welcoming parent volunteers, making positive phone calls home, and showing appreciation through notes and awards.

> **The more involved and positive parents are, the better their children will do in your class.**

Welcome Parent Volunteers

Many parents love to volunteer and have the time to do so on a regular basis. Other parents would also love to volunteer, but their full-time jobs make it difficult to schedule time to volunteer. Make the effort to invite all parents to volunteer in your classroom. You can do so at the beginning of the year at parent conferences or during back-to-school night. Take time to figure out when you really need help from parents, what their tasks will be, and what days and times you need them.

Another way to ask for parent volunteers during the year is to send home a "Calling for a Little Help" note (Figure 7.2) that simply describes the upcoming activity, the time and date, and the fact that you are looking for parent volunteers. Parents can return the paper if they are able to help.

Figure 7.2   Calling for a Little Help

Dear Parent,

Our class could use a set of helping hands. We hope you can help. Here is what we need:

_____

_____

_____

_____

_____

Yes! I can help!

_____

_____

_____

_____

_____

_____

Signature   Date   Phone

Make Positive Phone Calls Home

Most parents hear from teachers only when their children have misbehaved or performed poorly. A very powerful way to connect with parents is to pick up the phone occasionally and call parents just to tell them that their child is doing well in your class. Report to parents when their child has been a good friend to another student, improved grades, turned in homework regularly, or shown improvement in a specific area.

If you are a secondary teacher, you may find it more difficult to connect with parents due to the sheer numbers of students and parents you have. Yet you should try to call home when you notice a student could use some positive reinforcement or when you know parents are trying hard to support their child. Your efforts will go a long way.

> **Pick up the phone occasionally and call parents just to tell them that their child is doing well in your class.**

Show Appreciation Through Notes and Awards

Send parents notes of appreciation or awards when you sense that they truly support their children or your efforts in the classroom. Parents don't hear many positive things about their role, and a little note or award for their role will be long remembered and valued.

TAKE CARE OF YOURSELF ■

As you work in the teaching profession helping, advising, guiding, building relationships, and teaching students, you find that like other jobs, teaching has its share of stressful situations. Teaching is a giving profession; each day that you walk into your classroom, you are asked to give everything you have to your students. Therefore, taking care of yourself is critical.

Taking care of yourself means different things to different people. For many, it means living a balanced and healthy life. It might mean eating right, exercising, and enjoying interests and activities outside teaching. It might mean actively participating in a religious organization or volunteering in the community. It might be choosing to go home before grading papers to spend time with your family. It might be taking a weekend away without any schoolwork or reading a good book late into the night. Whatever it means to you, taking care of yourself must be high on your priority list. Teachers who don't take time to care for themselves will find themselves used up and exhausted within the first few years of teaching. Taking care of yourself is especially important because job demands grow each year. Barth, author of *Improving Schools From Within* (1990), illuminates this trend:

> I think there is a message here for those of us who work in schools. Over the years, we have assumed small, discrete additions to our responsibilities; for the safe passage of children from their homes to school; for ensuring that the sidewalks are plowed of snow; for maintaining the physical condition of the building. We have taken

on responsibility for children's achievement of minimal standards at each grade level; responsibility for children with special needs, for the gifted, and for those who are neither; and responsibility for administering tests, trying to ensure that as many children as possible score above average, and reporting the scores to the public. Not one of those responsibilities is backbreaking in itself, but collectively they present an enormous burden that is perhaps many times greater than we were designed for or are capable of sustaining. But like the locomotive in "The Little Engine That Could," we keep trying and puffing, "I think I can, I think I can." (p. 7)

Taking care of yourself must be high on your priority list.

In order to thrive and survive in this profession, it is crucial to use strong stress management techniques such as taking care of your emotional health, getting enough sleep, eating right, and exercising. Your body and mind need these things to rejuvenate themselves.

┌─ Potential Teaching Stressors ─┐

➤ Paperwork, paperwork, paperwork

➤ Accountability pressures (high-stakes exams, covering all the standards, etc.)

➤ Testing results going public; teachers and schools being compared with one another

➤ Lack of planning time

➤ Too many students in class

➤ Administrators who do not support you

➤ Inclusion of special education students in your class without the necessary support

➤ Being evaluated and observed

➤ Demanding curriculum: too much to cover and not enough time

➤ Lack of parental involvement or too much involvement

➤ Misbehavior by students

➤ Colleagues who are unprofessional

➤ Negative news reports regarding education

Emotional Health: The Foundation of Effective Teaching

Teaching is one of the most emotionally charged professions in the world. To spend each day around different personalities and to interact with unpredictable situations all day is not only exciting but very stressful. Some days, no matter how much planning you have done, nothing seems to flow right. Learning how to handle stress is essential. After a particularly stressful day, try fun-filled leisure activities such as going for a walk, seeing a movie, or playing a game. These activities help you separate yourself from the situation and clear your head.

Stress doesn't just go away, but if you are aware of what causes you stress on the job, you can avoid, ignore, or deal with these stressors. A teacher's life will never be stress- or problem-free. Yet by reflecting on those things that cause you stress, you can learn to counteract these stressors. Your emotional health is one of your most prized possessions; guard it, protect it, own it, embrace it, and, most of all, love it.

Balanced Living: Sleep, Nutrition, and Exercise

Before you can focus on teaching well each day, you must care for your own basic needs. For most people, that means getting enough sleep, eating the right foods, and exercising. For others it is participating in religious activities, practicing yoga, and spending more time with family. Recognizing and fulfilling your own needs helps you work smarter, not harder, and makes teaching more fulfilling.

Sleep Debt Bank Account

Everyone has a sleep debt bank account. Many teachers have weeks in which grading papers, writing notes home, filing, completing report cards, and other miscellaneous time snatchers keep them awake past their bedtime. In fact, one of the most challenging times for teachers is the week before school begins and the first few weeks of school. You have much to do to prepare for the year, and you put a lot of energy into starting the year off right with students and parents. You may quickly find yourself exhausted and sleep deprived, and the school year has hardly started! During this time, it is important to remember that you must maintain your personal sleep bank account by depositing consistent hours of sleep into the account. Consider depositing at least 8 hours of sleep for each 16-hour day of alertness. Start your year off right by depositing the right amount of sleep into your account. You will quickly find that you will be more alert and have more energy to show for it, and your school year will be off to a successful start.

Sleep: The Teacher's Saving Grace

It is stunning that more than 50% of Americans are sleep deprived. Consequently, it is likely that 50% of American teachers are sleep deprived. Even though most people know that sleep is important, sleep is the first thing to go when people get busy. Most people recognize that if they don't get enough sleep, the quality of their lives decreases, as does the quality of their teaching.

A very impressive book that addresses sleep is *Power Sleep* (Maas, 1999). In this book, Maas argues that in order to be fully alert, mentally sharp, creative, and energetic all day, people need to spend at least one third of their lives sleeping. He calculated that over a lifetime, people should spend nearly 24 years in bed.

The benefits of sleep are overwhelming. It makes people feel better, stronger, and sharper. Everyone has experienced those days when he or she felt drained and foggy headed after a bad night's sleep. For workers in any profession, these days are not productive. For someone working in a profession like teaching—a profession that requires you to bring all your mental, physical, social, and emotional talent and strength to the classroom each day—sleep becomes even more critical. Teachers are asked to be fully alert for 6–7 straight hours—managing students, answering questions, making decisions at lightning speed. In some professions, tired employees can hide behind a computer screen and mumble now and then. For teachers, sleep is the foundation of their effectiveness and fulfillment in the classroom. Figure 7.3 highlights the benefits of a good night's sleep.

For teachers, sleep is the foundation of their effectiveness and fulfillment in the classroom.

Figure 7.3   The Benefits of Sleep

- ❏ Restores and heals the body
- ❏ Bolsters the immune system
- ❏ Helps in memory storage, retention, and reorganization
- ❏ Is crucial to new learning and retention

Maas recommends several ways to improve your sleeping habits. First, strive to go to bed at the same time every night, even on the weekend. A regular sleeping pattern helps your body get into a routine of sleep. Second, establish a bedtime ritual. For example, you might read before going to sleep, write in a journal, or watch the evening news. These rituals help take your mind off the day's events and allow you to drift off into drowsiness.

Nutrition and Water: Sustaining Energy

This is not a book on nutrition. However, we must mention that it is important for you to realize that everything you put into your body affects how you relate to your students. Those fun-loving and energetic kids with whom you spend your days keep you accountable on many levels: You can't go without meals or you'll bite their heads off. You can't eat pure sugar or you will quickly bounce off the walls and come crashing down with little or no energy.

When you eat right, your moods stay balanced, and you feel much more in control. When you eat poorly or skip meals, you are left with headaches, irritation, mood swings, and exhaustion. Take the time to pack a good lunch. Many nutrition experts recommend keeping lunch light. A low-fat lunch that contains approximately 500–600 calories maintains afternoon alertness and boosts energy levels.

Keep a bottle of water on your desk at all times as well. The experts recommend drinking at least eight glasses of water each day. The brain is 70% water and needs constant refreshment. In addition, water cleans out your body and gets rid of those unwanted hormones and bacteria, helping you stay healthy. Drinking water helps reduce fatigue, improves skin color and tone, and keeps your digestive system working properly.

The Exercising Teacher

Exercise reduces stress and generally makes people healthier. Exercise increases the brain's production of endorphins, and endorphins act as natural mood elevators. Exercise can reduce pain, relax muscles, suppress appetite, and produce feelings of general well-being. It increases blood flow throughout the body, and since blood carries oxygen, it also increases the amount of oxygen getting to the muscles and the brain. Exercise helps joints remain flexible and muscles get stronger. It reduces the likelihood of heart disease and stroke. It also reduces stress and anxiety and boosts the body's natural defenses against health-damaging stress hormones.

Teaching lends itself to an active lifestyle. In contrast to all the jobs in which workers sit at a desk for hours on end, most teachers stand and walk during most of the day. They sprint across campus to arrive in their classrooms on time or dash to the office for a quick bathroom break. The life of the teacher begins by being physically fit. Teaching to your potential requires physical stamina and endurance.

With this in mind, it is crucial that you keep yourself in good physical shape. It does not matter how big or small or how strong or weak you are. It doesn't matter if you like physical education or not. What matters is that you exercise your body on a regular basis. The more you exercise, the less exhausted you will be at the end of the

> **The more you exercise, the more you increase your physical strength and endurance.**

day because you will increase your physical strength and endurance. You don't have to run marathons. Just start off small and keep going. For example, walk twice a week at lunch or after school, visit the nearby gym and watch the news while riding a stationary bike, or spend a few dollars and buy a treadmill.

A LAST LOOK AT THE TEACHER AS A RELATIONSHIP BUILDER ■

Building relationships with students and parents is a key to being a successful and effective teacher. By putting thought and time into these relationships, you will build relationships that foster learning by offering emotional support and caring. Certain students will always challenge you, and by learning how best to deal with these individuals, you can conserve your energy as you work effectively with them. Strive to understand what makes your students and parents tick, and you will be amazed at how you can transform your classroom into a true community of learners.

RECOMMENDED READINGS ■

Barth, R. (2003). *Lessons learned: Shaping relationships and the culture of the workplace.* Thousand Oaks, CA: Corwin Press.

Canter & Associates. (1998). *First class teacher: Successful strategies for new teachers.* Santa Monica, CA: Author.

Goleman, D. (1995). *Emotional intelligence.* New York: Bantam.

Palmer, P. (1998). *The courage to teach: Exploring the inner landscape of a teacher's life.* San Francisco: Jossey-Bass.

Wooden, J. (2004). *My personal best: Life lessons from an all-American journey.* New York: McGraw-Hill.

Questions for Reflection

What strategies do I use to connect with students?

_____

_____

_____

How can I best support students who are having a difficult time in school?

_____

_____

_____

Which students must I make an extra effort to connect with?

_____

_____

_____

How can I better communicate with parents what their children are learning in my class?

_____

_____

_____

How can parents support learning at home?

_____

_____

_____

Teacher as a Communicator

"HOW DO I STAY IN TOUCH WITH PARENTS AND THE LARGER SCHOOL COMMUNITY?"

One critical skill that continues to develop throughout your teaching career is communication. If your communication skills are strong, your teaching will be strong. Your students will know what they are supposed to be doing, your parents will know why you are doing what you are doing, and your principal will feel comfortable with your curriculum and management decisions. Teachers communicate with several audiences: students, parents or guardians, administrators, mentors, classified staff (office managers, secretaries, custodians), paraprofessionals, volunteers, and community members.

Figure 8.1 shows the three basic traits of a great communicator. First, great communicators can *clearly articulate* their message by using both verbal and nonverbal skills. Great communicators begin by knowing what they want to communicate and then delivering the message in a clear and direct way that helps the listener understand the message. Second, great communicators are *good listeners* who understand their audience. Third, great communicators *use a variety of communication styles* to fit their audience because they realize that not everyone can hear the message in the same way. A great communicator can communicate well through writing (using proper grammar, sentence structure, and spelling) and speaking (using effective expressions and gestures to drive home points or make other, more subtle points within a discussion).

Figure 8.1   A Great Communicator

❑ Can clearly articulate his or her message
❑ Is a good listener
❑ Uses a variety of communication styles

■ COMMUNICATING EFFECTIVELY WITH PARENTS

Parents (and guardians) are your second-most-important audience (after your students). Happy parents can be your strongest fans and advocates. Unhappy parents can make your year difficult. Do everything possible to ensure that you build positive relationships with parents.

Before we discuss how best to communicate with parents, we must acknowledge that it is impossible to please every parent. Teachers are often confronted with parents who are unhappy about a teacher, course, or technique used in school. Effective communication between you and parents is often the best answer to handling any and all problems. Figure 8.2 highlights sound suggestions for establishing strong and effective relationships with parents. Each of the suggestions is discussed in the following paragraphs.

• *Strive to become partners.* Make it clear that you cannot do your job without help from the home. When teachers and parents work together, they demonstrate to students that they are teamed together to help the student reach his or her potential. You can learn a great deal about students by listening carefully to what parents have to say.

Figure 8.2   Communicating Effectively With Parents

- ❑ Strive to become partners.
- ❑ Avoid surprises.
- ❑ Use proactive communication.
- ❑ Keep a parent communication log.
- ❑ Welcome parent involvement.
- ❑ Stay informed.
- ❑ Explain stages of growth.
- ❑ Encourage parents to communicate with you.

• *Avoid surprises.* Surprises are best kept for birthdays and other special occasions. Parents should never be surprised by a report card grade or comment. Likewise, they should not be surprised by curricular content.

• *Use proactive communication.* Some teachers hesitate to telephone parents about academic and behavior problems. However, if they do contact parents, they often spare themselves problems later. By keeping parents informed, teachers and administrators show initiative about what students need to be successful in school. When parents call about a problem, teachers are often put in a defensive position as they explain why they haven't informed parents of a developing situation.

• *Keep a parent communication log.* Begin by noting the date and time you talked with the parent, the general topic, and then details of what was discussed. This will allow you to refer to previous conversations as the year unfolds, as well as document your effort to include parents in your classroom.

• *Welcome parent involvement.* Parents who get involved with school projects or serve as resources feel more like a part of the school and are better able to understand the problems faced by teachers and

Tips for Communicating Through Writing

1. Be certain that your written communications with parents are accurate and professional.
2. Keep a record of all written communication to parents or school personnel. Keep a copy of every document in a folder.
3. Make all notes, permission slips, reports, requests, and explanations of school activities easy to read and understand.
4. Avoid errors in grammar and spelling.
5. Write clearly and concisely so that parents will understand your message. Be accurate with times, dates, and locations.
6. Avoid education jargon.
7. Send your written communication far enough in advance so that parents can act.
8. Ask a colleague to read your written communication before you send it to see whether it can be improved.
9. Give a copy of your parent communications to your administrator.

Fostering Communication With Parents of Second Language Learners

➢ Translate written communications.
➢ Use an interpreter.
➢ Give the gift of time.
➢ Avoid stereotypes.
➢ Share space appropriately.
➢ Use culturally sensitive eye contact.

students. Many parents can help by using their talents to enhance the classroom environment and activities.

• *Stay informed.* When an upset parent calls or comes to the school, try to find out what the problem might be before talking with the parent. Even a little input may help. Check your grade books and think about the student's recent difficulties with assignments, behavior, and peer interaction. Review the student's standardized test scores, absence record, and items of interest in a student's file.

• *Explain stages of growth.* Hold meetings with parent groups early in a school year. Explain to parents what they may expect of their children at certain ages and describe peer problems and behavioral changes that students might face. Some students experience social problems with their peers. Unpleasant peer incidents sometimes happen when teachers and administrators are not watching.

• *Encourage parents to communicate with you.* Establishing ongoing communication with parents helps you do your job better. Use handwritten, typed, or e-mailed notes to communicate with parents. Consider jotting notes into students' assignment booklets on a regular basis, thereby facilitating an ongoing "conversation" with parents throughout the school year. See the sidebar on page 163 titled "Tips for Communicating Through Writing" for more ideas.

Communicating With Parents of Second Language Learners

Many students across the United States are learning English as a second language. This offers exciting challenges and some struggles for teachers. One of the more challenging aspects of working with English language learners is finding ways to communicate with their parents, many of whom do not speak English themselves. Many of these parents are intimidated by the school system and often do not become actively involved in their children's education because of language issues. It is up to you to welcome them into the school setting and to help them realize that they are an important part of the school community. Keep the following ideas in mind as you try to foster communication with parents of English learners:

• *Translate written communications.* Send messages home in the parents' native language when possible. Find someone who can translate your letters into the parents' native language.

• *Use an interpreter.* When you schedule meetings with parents, bring in an interpreter to facilitate two-way communication between you and the parents. Promote parents' participation by being courteous and sincere and by offering ample opportunity and time to convey concerns.

• *Give the gift of time.* Provide ample opportunity for parents to respond. Try to resist the temptation to interrupt or to fill silences. If a parent is formulating a response and has not answered promptly, don't assume the delay represents a lack of interest in responding.

• *Avoid stereotypes.* Keep in mind that families from different cultures have different and unique cultural styles. Remember that no set of characteristics can be ascribed to all members of any ethnic group. The cultural traits of individuals range from those traditionally attributed to the ethnic group to those ascribed to the newly assimilated culture.

- *Share space appropriately.* People from different cultures use, value, and share space differently. In some cultures it is considered appropriate for people to stand very close to each other while talking, whereas in other cultures people like to stand farther apart. Keep this in mind when working with parents from other cultures.

- *Use culturally sensitive eye contact.* Be aware that in some cultures it is customary for the listener to avert the eyes, whereas in other cultures it is customary to make direct eye contact while listening.

> ## Worthwhile Web Sites
>
> The following Web sites will help you as you work with parents of second language learners:
>
> **Everything ESL** (www.everythingesl.net)
>
> **Humanizing Language Teaching** (www.hltmag.co.uk)

MAKING YOUR BACK-TO-SCHOOL NIGHT A SUCCESS

Many schools offer parents a preparatory open house at the beginning of the school year. Often called "back-to-school night," it is one of the most important events on the school calendar. During this time you can set the tone for the entire year with the parents of your new students. This event can open the door to communication, trust, and cooperation. You have the opportunity to share your goals, expectations, credentials, classroom rules and policies, and philosophies in one short presentation.

Whether you are a brand-new teacher or a veteran of many years, back-to-school night can be stressful. Careful and thorough preparation will help you present yourself with confidence and clarity. Figure 8.3 provides a checklist of details that should be considered when preparing for this big night.

Figure 8.3   Back-to-School-Night Checklist

❑ Is your room orderly, clean, and easy to walk around?

❑ Do you have extra chairs?

❑ Are students' names and work samples clearly displayed on their desks?

❑ Do you have a sign-in sheet? Volunteer sign-up sheet?

❑ Are you dressed professionally?

❑ Is your daily schedule available to parents?

❑ Do you know how you are going to explain the curriculum?

❑ Are you ready to discuss how students will be assessed, both formally and informally, during the year?

❑ Do you have suggestions for ways parents can help their children at home?

❑ Do you have your discipline and homework information ready for parents?

Preparing for Back-to-School Night

You will definitely feel more relaxed if you have everything in place for back-to-school night. Remember, the main purpose of the evening is to proactively inform parents about the year ahead for their child. Parents need to leave your classroom feeling that their child is in capable hands and will be academically challenged and personally respected.

Master Names

During the first week of school, practice the first and last names of your students until you feel entirely comfortable pronouncing all of them. Remember that students' and parents' last names are not necessarily the same. Some students may live with adults other than their parents or have parents who have remarried. Take the time to learn the proper name associations for your class.

Look Fresh

If you do not have time to go home between school and back-to-school night, bring clothes to change into. You'll feel better if you take some time to freshen up. Be well groomed and dress appropriately. Remember, these children are their parents' most precious possessions, so the parents need to trust you. If you look messy or disheveled, parents won't be willing to place their confidence in you.

Energize Yourself

Be sure to have something to eat and take a few minutes to sit down and relax between the school day and back-to-school night. You will need this energy to sustain you in the hours ahead.

Straighten Your Classroom

Make the room look organized and inviting. Ask students to clean their desks before the end of the day. Hide the extra piles of paper and empty the trash.

Provide Ample Seating

Bring in extra chairs. It is unnerving and uninviting to ask parents to stand or to rush around looking for chairs at the last minute.

Prepare Materials

Make sure to organize any handouts, forms, or overheads ahead of time. Ask a colleague to proof them, and have plenty on hand.

Provide a Visual Outline

Create an overview of the units of study on the blackboard or overhead so that you can discuss it with parents. If you normally write a daily schedule on the board, use it as a reference to help you stay focused during your presentation.

Label Desks

Be sure students' names are clearly marked on their desks. Ask parents to sit at their child's desk. Parents enjoy experiencing your room as their children do, and having them in their child's seat will help you remember who is who.

Allow for Parent Feedback

Give parents an index card or sheet to tell you anything they would like you to know about their child (e.g., interests, fears, concerns, anything they feel is important). This information is invaluable.

Give Student Letters to Parents

Ask students to write a letter to their parents during the day welcoming them to the class. Leave these letters on the desks for parents to enjoy when they arrive. Encourage parents to respond and to leave their response on the desk for the children to find the next morning.

Review Student Work

Place on each child's desk the textbooks that the students will use during the school year so that the parents can see them and ask questions. Ask students to leave their journals, portfolios, or other work on their desk for parents to review.

Discuss Homework Policy

Write a homework policy letter for your classroom. Place a copy of the letter on each child's desk for parents to take home. (Also include this letter in the take-home envelope sent the first week of school.) The letter should explain when homework is due, how it is checked, and your policies for late assignments. To give yourself ideas if you are a new teacher, ask several colleagues to show you copies of their policies.

Explain Discipline Policy

Write a discipline policy letter for your classroom. Place a copy on each child's desk for parents to take home. Explain how your classroom discipline policy works. Familiarize parents with the school's discipline policy and how it may affect their child.

Starting the Evening Off Right

If you have thoroughly prepared for back-to-school night, you should be ready to meet parents. Keep in mind the following suggestions to get the evening off on the right foot.

Make a Good First Impression

As parents enter your classroom, introduce yourself and allow parents to introduce themselves. Try to remember which child goes with which parent. Do your best to make verbal contact with each parent before you begin your presentation.

Be Punctual

Be in your classroom, ready to go, one-half hour before the starting time. Some parents will arrive early, and you must be ready for them.

Take Time for Introductions

Begin the presentation by introducing yourself—your full name and your experience with children in student teaching, summer camps, tutoring, and so on. If this is your first year teaching, you do not need to tell parents so if it makes you feel uncomfortable. If parents ask, a simple yes will suffice. Be sure to introduce assistants, aides, or student teachers who are working with your class. (Ask them to be present if at all possible. Students will also work with these people, and it is important for the parents to get to know them as well.)

Follow Your Agenda

Work your way through the school day using the schedule you have written on the board as a reference. Clearly outline what students will learn in each curriculum area.

Highlight the Grading System

Go over the school's grading system for your grade level. Be sure to explain the school's grading policy and how you will implement it in the classroom. It is very important to present this topic clearly and correctly. You will most likely be asked several questions about grading policies.

Provide Time for Questions

Be sure to pause for questions and answers at several points in your presentation. Before you move on to the next topic, ask the parents if they feel clear about what you have said so far. Conclude your presentation with a final chance for parents to ask questions. If you don't know the answer to a question, say "I don't know, but I will see what I can find out and get back to you." Write the question down so parents see that their concerns are important to you.

Discuss Parent-Teacher Communication

Let the parents know how to contact you and what form of communication they will receive from you (e.g., weekly newsletter, e-mails, monthly calendar, Web site). Share your e-mail address if e-mail is an option.

Brain Bits

When giving an oral presentation, it is important to "chunk" information so listeners can remember the information you are attempting to convey. Chunking is the process by which a large amount of information is classified into various categories. According to Sousa in *How the Brain Learns*, Third edition (2006), chunking can raise learning, thinking, and retention of information significantly. Therefore, instead of giving parents or students a laundry list of information, organize your presentations into several large categories. For back-to-school night, this may include categories such as classroom management (rules, procedures, consequences, rewards, etc.), curriculum (textbooks, state standards, etc.), and assessment (grading, homework policy, state exam information, progress reports, etc.).

Finish on Time

Parents have families and babysitters waiting at home. Be sure to finish on time. Be as gracious as possible to parents who linger afterward. Suggest you walk out together.

PARENT CONFERENCES ■

After parents are introduced to your classroom during back-to-school night, the next important step is to establish a two-way line of communication with each student's family. When parents and teachers work together, students achieve higher test scores and grades and demonstrate positive behavior and attitudes, all of which can result in improved long-term academic achievement. At the beginning of the school year, take the opportunity to contact your students' parents. This can be accomplished through a letter of introduction, a telephone conversation, an e-mail, or a newsletter.

One of the most critical activities you will do all year is to meet with a student's parents. If this conference goes well, then you will gain the parents' support and loyalty for the remainder of the year. If the conference doesn't go well, then you will spend the remainder of the year repairing the relationship with those parents.

When to Initiate a Conference

Parent conferences can be held for many different reasons and at many different times. Many teachers are required to meet or choose to meet with parents in the beginning of the school year to set learning goals, discuss the year's plans, and share ongoing assessments. We might call these conferences *beginning-of-the-year parent conferences*. Other teachers choose to meet with parents to share concerns or problems that have arisen in class. We might call these conferences *addressing-a-problem parent conferences*. Both types of conferences are discussed in the following sections. For both types, you may use the Parent Conference Planning Form (Figure 8.4) and the Parent Conference Checklist (Figure 8.5) to help you plan a smooth and successful parent conference.

Beginning-of-the-Year Parent Conferences

A positive beginning-of-the-year parent conference can set the stage for a great school year for everyone involved. Following are some suggestions to help make the beginning-of-the-year conferences a success.

Plan Carefully

Successful parent-teacher conferences are the result of careful planning. Know what you want to discuss with the parents before the conference. Jot down notes or prepare an agenda to follow.

Figure 8.4   Parent Conference Planning Form

Student's Name: _____

Parents' Names: _____

Conference Date and Time: _____

Reason for Conference: _____

  1. Student's academic strengths:

  2. Student's academic weaknesses that must be addressed:

  3. Student's academic goals for the remainder of year:

  4. Parent input on academic issues:

  5. Student's social strengths:

  6. Student's social weaknesses that must be addressed:

  7. Student's unique gifts and talents:

  8. Past problems to be updated at conference:

  9. Additional issues parents wish to discuss:

  10. Additional conference notes:

Figure 8.5   Parent Conference Checklist

Have you prepared:

❑ Schedule, agenda, or talking points?

❑ Student work folders?

❑ Specific student data and behavioral information?

❑ Seating, waiting, and conference areas (adult-sized chairs around a table)?

❑ Student self-assessments?

❑ Written expectations for student work and behavior?

❑ Personalized comments or observations for each student?

❑ Suggestions for home activities?

❑ Preconference surveys for parents to identify their agenda items? (This optional survey can be sent home a week before conferences and provides an avenue for parents to voice concerns or topics so that you can be better prepared and less surprised.)

❑ Copies of curriculum and standards?

❑ Behavioral or homework policies or both?

❑ Refreshments (e.g., coffee, hot water and teabags, sugar, creamer, cups, napkins)?

❑ Pens, pencils, paper?

Have you consulted the student's cumulative folder?

Make Parents Feel Comfortable

Tell parents positive things about their child. Help them realize that you want to work with them as a team to support their child. Put yourself in the parents' shoes. Choose your words carefully—think about how you would feel if you were the parent hearing certain information from a teacher. Avoid upsetting the parents.

Be Prepared

Be sure that you have the student's grades and work samples, copies of notes sent home, and copies of any office referrals. Keep this information handy by creating a folder for each student or using a notebook with dividers for each student. Use an organization system that allows you to keep individual student information handy, organized, and accessible.

Consult the Cumulative Folder

Before the conference, check the cumulative folder of any student who is having difficulty with academics or social adjustment. This will allow you to ascertain important information about the student's background; acquaint you with recommendations from previous teachers, testing agencies, or doctors; inform you of legal or medical matters; discover the student's previous standardized test scores and grades; and much more.

Share Curriculum and Standards

Carefully outline what the child is going to be studying this year and what your expectations for homework and study skills are. Discuss your standards with parents and provide them with a copy of these standards.

Talk Only About Their Child

Stay focused on the parents' child and the progress he or she is making. Do not compare the child to siblings or other students in the class.

Suggest Home Activities

Give suggestions for activities parents can do at home with their child that will support their child's educational program. Your suggestions can include practical activities for helping children learn concepts they are being taught in the classroom. For example, parents might cook with their child to reinforce fractions or create a collage of family pictures to discuss different generations.

Be Warm

Introduce yourself in a warm manner, no matter what you think of the student. You set the tone. The parents should feel comfortable and feel that you are glad they came to the conference.

Stay on Schedule

If your school schedules conferences back-to-back, stick to your conference times. People become annoyed when they are forced to wait. If you need to continue a conference and it is time to move on to the next conference, say, "Let's schedule a time to continue because I must move on to my next conference." When a parent has two or more children at the school, work with your colleagues to leave one time slot between sibling conferences so that the parent has plenty of time to get from one room to the other and you can stay on schedule.

Refer to the Administrator

If parents have questions that you cannot answer about issues such as test scores, textbooks, or other problems, ask them to see the school administrator.

Wrap Up Positively

Conclude your conference in a positive manner. Let parents know that education is a partnership between the home and the school for the good of the child. Review any solutions or courses of action that you and the parents discussed and agreed to.

Thank the Parents

Remember to thank parents for attending the conference and for being so involved in their child's education. Make sure they know that by being involved in their child's education, they are ensuring that their child will have the support needed to achieve at his or her highest level. Assure them that this conference isn't the only time they can hear how their child is doing or communicate with you. Inform them of the various ways you will be sending home information and the easiest way to contact you if they have a question or concern.

Addressing-a-Problem Parent Conferences

Calling a parent conference to discuss a problem or an issue is never easy. Yet because these conferences are proactive, they can often lead to solutions and improvement in student behavior and attitudes. As general advice, strive to always be positive in all communications with parents. Be an active listener so parents feel what they are saying is important. Avoid labeling students as bad; instead label the behavior that needs adjustment. Last, acknowledge parents as the expert and a partner in their child's education success and work together to find a solution. Follow these suggestions to organize a parent conference to address a problem.

Initiating the Conference

Before holding a conference or making a phone call to address a problem or an issue, take a few minutes to jot down a few notes. The prompts included in Figure 8.6 can help guide your discussion and keep you on track.

Figure 8.6   Parent Conference Form

Parent Conference Form for _____

1. Statement of concern:

2. Specific problem or behavior:

3. Steps taken so far to address problem:

4. Parental input on problem (if any):

5. Ideas for solutions:

6. Expected follow-up activities:

Watch What You Say

It's not a good idea to say something like, "This is a pretty bad class, and when your child acts up, it just makes things more difficult for me." Even if you have a challenging class, giving parents the impression that you are having classroom management problems won't help you. Instead, stay focused on their child and their child only.

Find Something Positive

Even when addressing a problem, always make sure to tell parents something positive about their child; there are many wonderful things to say about every child. Begin the conference on a positive note. For example, you might say, "Mr. Jones, Lee is a very positive student in class and usually follows the classroom rules. Yet it seems that when he is on the playground, he has some problems following rules." Or you might say, "Mrs. Griffin, Sarah is a very helpful student in class and is frequently asking what she can do to help me. However, it seems as though Sarah is really struggling when it comes to completing her math homework. I am wondering if you have noticed the same thing at home?"

Check the Cumulative Folder

Make notes of previous problems indicated in the student's cumulative file. If you teach at the secondary level, you might ask a counselor or dean if the student has been referred for disciplinary or academic problems by other teachers. Use this information to examine patterns with the parents or to remind them of past occurrences.

Ask Open-Ended Questions

Asking questions of the parent helps parents share valuable and critical information about the student. It also helps parents vent their feelings and emotions. Asking open-ended questions provides an environment in which there are no right or wrong answers. These are questions such as, What do you feel Kim's strengths and weaknesses in previous years have been? or, In your opinion, what type of classroom environment has Victor thrived in? If you allow parents to offer up their thoughts, opinions, and suggestions, they can feel they are part of the solution and a valuable member of the team.

Avoid Putting the Parent on the Defensive

Be objective, not subjective. Stay away from psychological explanations of a student's academic or social problems. Tell the parents the facts of the situations in class and describe how the child has responded. Explain social problems without naming other students. Talk about a child who is very active in class by describing behaviors. If parents ask whether this is normal behavior, explain that you have observed many children and the behavior is unique, but that you, the parents, and the child can work together to help the child. Be honest and direct and explain difficulties clearly so that parents understand.

Avoid Making Judgments

Don't jump to conclusions about a student's ability unless you know what you are talking about. Avoid saying, "Pete has outstanding ability and is not working up to his potential" if Pete's records do not indicate this. Teachers like to encourage parents, but statements such as this may give the parents false hopes. Instead of referring to ability, say, "Helen is not achieving as I expect in math. On her tests she does not demonstrate mastery of the material, but in class she often makes excellent responses. I suggest that if she would study more at home and organize her papers, I can help her improve her test-taking skills. Let's work together to help her perform better on her tests."

Address Eyesight and Hearing Issues

Recommend that parents rule out problems with eyesight and hearing early on by talking to the family doctor about the child's symptoms. Check with the school nurse to see whether the child's eyesight or hearing has been tested. If it has, make sure that the parents are aware of the testing and the results.

> ### ─ Brain Bits ──
>
> The primacy effect, discussed in *How the Brain Learns*, Third edition (2006), refers to the order of information presented in conversation and how well that information is remembered. Research shows that the brain remembers best what is said first and last; what is said in the middle of a conversation is more likely to be forgotten.

Accept the Prospect of No Solution

Not all problems have corresponding solutions. Many problems have deep-seated causes. Solving every problem is not possible. Your role is to demonstrate to the parent what you have experienced with the child.

Refer to a Specialist

If parents ask whether the child has a learning problem such as ADD, ADHD, or dyslexia, explain that you aren't qualified to determine this but that you and the school are happy to work to meet the needs of the student. If indicated, make a referral to school personnel who are able to identify the student's special needs. If the parents are working with specialists from private organizations, indicate your willingness to work with them. In any case, be sure to understand your school's procedures and guidelines before proceeding.

Communicate With School Administrators

Let school administrators know of any problems you experience in your conferences. If the conference becomes hostile, ask for an end to the meeting, move the conference to the administrator's office, or ask for a break and go to the office or restroom to collect yourself. Encourage parents to state their complaints against you in writing. If you expect that the conference will be difficult, ask a school administrator to sit in on the conference.

ONGOING COMMUNICATION   ■

Parent conferences and back-to-school nights provide formal opportunities to communicate with parents. It is also important to have less formal communication avenues to keep parents involved and engaged in their child's education. These avenues can include classroom newsletters, classroom Web pages, and e-mail.

A Great Way to Introduce Yourself

A great way to introduce yourself and communicate your excitement about the year ahead is to send home a short letter or newsletter on the first day of school. You can include a section about yourself, what college you attended, why you chose to become a teacher, your hobbies, and so forth. You can also include your goals for the year and important dates such as back-to-school night, parent conferences, and other school functions. You might throw in your e-mail address to give parents a feeling that you want to be in touch with them right from the start.

Writing Classroom Newsletters

Classroom newsletters are an excellent way to keep in touch with parents and to help them take part in their child's education. Regular class newsletters help parents feel involved in class activities and gain insights into what their child is learning.

What Should I Include in a Newsletter?

➤ Mini-surveys
➤ Message from the teacher
➤ Classroom visitors
➤ Upcoming events
➤ Lesson of the week
➤ Samples of student work
➤ Parent education information
➤ Student art

Newsletters can include curriculum topics, samples of student work, and parent education information. They can provide up-to-date news about upcoming events and curriculum areas as well as recent student accomplishments.

Classroom newsletters can be designed in a variety of forms. No matter what format you choose, be sure to keep it simple so you can continue using the newsletter as a communication tool.

If possible, translate the letter into other languages if English is not spoken in the students' homes. Ask a volunteer or parent to do the translation. If it is not possible to translate the newsletter, be sure to review it with students and ask them to explain the information in it to their parents.

You may choose to create a teacher-written or student-written newsletter. The primary goal of a teacher-written newsletter is to communicate with parents on a regular basis. The format of this written communication can range from a traditional newsletter to a weekly lesson plan to a monthly calendar. Start slow and small. Choose a newsletter format that will not take too much of your time; if your format is complicated, you will dread working on it in the busy months ahead. Make your newsletter simple and direct. Allow it to act as your teacher's aide, preparing parents for upcoming events and eliminating surprises about progress reports, report cards, and testing.

You may choose to involve students in creating a student-written newsletter. Creating a newsletter engages students in a meaningful writing activity. Since a primary goal of the newsletter is to communicate with parents, the student-written newsletter should reflect this goal. For ideas on what parents might like to hear about, see the sidebar on page 176 titled "What Should I Include in a Newsletter?"

Designing Classroom Web Sites

One of the great advantages of being a teacher today is the ability to use Web pages and e-mail to facilitate two-way communication between you and parents. One great option is to design your own classroom Web site for students and parents to visit for information about your classroom, assignments, and other topics. (See Figure 8.7 for tips on designing your site.) Ask your administrator to check the site before you post it. Your administrator must know what you have posted and may suggest additional items for your site. Remember that not all students have access to a computer or the Internet in their homes. Take time to help these students gain access in the school's lab or on the classroom computer before or after school.

Figure 8.7   Tips for Designing a Classroom Web Site

❑ Create pages that do not need frequent maintenance. (For example, be sure to include permanent items such as school and classroom policies, classroom materials used all year, background information about you, etc.)

❑ Create individual pages for information—grades, homework, assignments, and so on—that will be updated frequently. You might also include notes and practice problems for key units.

❑ For each course you teach, create a main page with links to other important pages.

❑ Link your individual pages to the main page. Remember to link your classroom Web site to your school's Web site.

Make your Web site complement your teaching. More and more teachers are learning the benefits of creating a classroom Web site. By answering frequently asked questions on the Web site, you can greatly reduce the number of phone calls from parents and redundant questions from students. You might also include the following on your Web site:

• *Lecture Notes.* When you post lecture notes, students can refer to them after the lecture and feel free to pay attention and contribute in classroom discussions without fear of missing the notes. Students can also print out the notes before the discussion and fill in details as the discussion unfolds.

• *Projects and Assignments.* You can post your assignments online as well as hand them out. Online assignments are handy for students who have forgotten to bring the assignment home or for parents who want to check which assignments are due.

Additional Items to Include on a Classroom Web Site

➤ Policies

➤ Class schedules

➤ Lunch menus

➤ General school information

➤ Information about yourself and your educational philosophy

➤ Makeup work (for absent students)

➤ Practice problems and quizzes

➤ Major projects (including rubrics that will be used for grading the projects)

➤ Student work and projects

• *Homework.* Posting homework biweekly, monthly, or by the unit can improve student planning and preparation. You can also select other Web sites you want your students to visit, link them to your assignment pages, and write a special assignment to correlate with the linked page.

• *Student Web Pages.* Students can create their own Web pages to display presentations or projects in a format that you can access easily. Encourage students who have computer access to work with students who don't have access in order to equalize the assignment.

The "Additional Items" sidebar lists more items you might include on your Web site.

Using E-Mail

Electronic mail—or e-mail—is used for anything that mail, special delivery, faxes, or telephones can deliver. E-mail continues to grow in popularity, and now it is rare to find individuals who do not use e-mail. E-mail is a networking vehicle. Despite the many tools available for accessing information over the Internet, for many people e-mail remains the most useful application. This is probably true because e-mail is not merely about information—it is about human communication.

If you have access to e-mail and know that some or the majority of your parents do as well, you might consider using e-mail for two-way communications. Begin by mentioning this option to parents during your fall conferences. If they agree that using e-mail would be beneficial, exchange e-mail addresses and let the communication begin.

Many types of information can be shared through e-mail:

Worthwhile Web Sites

The following Web sites offer online platforms for classrooms and other educational forums:

Blackboard.com (www.blackboard.com)

High School Internet Network (ihigh.com)

• *Classroom newsletters* can be sent as attachments to e-mail. Sending newsletters by e-mail ensures that parents receive them instead of their ending up in the bottom of students' backpacks.

• *Informal progress reports* (brief notes regarding the student's behavior or academic achievements) can be sent via e-mail. Progress reports can be positive or negative. In either case, these notes offer immediate feedback, and immediate feedback is a powerful tool.

- *Parent-student communication* can take place via e-mail. You may ask students to e-mail their parents about how they did in school that day. Use this technique to reward students (reports about good behavior or academic achievements) or to punish students (reports about misbehaving or not working in class).

- *Parents' questions or concerns* can be relayed through e-mail. Encourage parents to use e-mail rather than calling you during the school day. This allows you to answer their questions before or after school, when students are not present.

E-mail is a mixture of conversation and writing. Remember to use a professional tone when writing e-mails to parents. Check your grammar and spelling, and don't use slang.

COMMUNICATING WITH THE SCHOOL COMMUNITY AT LARGE

Part of being a good communicator is building solid relationships based on openness and honesty with other members of the school community. These individuals include administrators, mentors, classified staff, paraprofessionals, volunteers, and the community at large. Each of these relationships is governed by different parameters.

Administrators

Being a site administrator is a busy job. In the past, administrators had the desire and time to assist new teachers in becoming acclimated to teaching. However, many site administrators now report having the desire but not the time to support new teachers. This does not mean that your site administrators will not support you. It simply means that you need to look elsewhere for ongoing, daily support and refrain from approaching the principal or assistant principal with every little question or concern.

Take time to meet with site administrators in the beginning of the year, and do your best to let them get to know you as you get to know them. Try to figure out what is important to your principal and assistant principal and what they look for in their teachers. Remember that this relationship is a two-way street—you must support the administrators, just as they must support you. If you keep this in mind, you can build a strong and supportive relationship with school administrators.

Mentors

Probably the best advice any new teacher can receive is to find a mentor. If you are lucky enough to work in a district that offers a mentor program, then be sure to participate. If, however, your district does not have a mentor program, find your own mentor. Get acquainted with your colleagues and find someone you respect and feel you could learn from. Ask this teacher to consider mentoring you. Most veteran teachers will view this request as a compliment and will be willing to mentor you. Most veteran teachers remember how challenging their first year of teaching was and are happy to support new teachers.

After your mentor has agreed to work with you, feel free to approach him or her with questions, concerns, and ideas. Sound out your ideas and ask advice on ways to solve problems. Mentors understand the school culture and know how to approach administrators and others for resources and support. Be open to advice and constructive critiques from your mentor. Remember that your first year of teaching is all about learning, not about impressing others with how good you already are. *The best teachers are humble teachers.*

Classified Staff

Some of the most important people in your life are the school's office manager, secretaries, and custodians. Take the time to get to know them. Ask them questions about their own lives. These individuals spend much of their day answering questions and helping others solve problems. They will be appreciative if you are interested in them as people, not just as people who can help you.

Relationships with staff are a two-way street. Try to figure out how you can help them as well as how they can help you. The custodian might really appreciate it if you place the trash cans near the door, or the school secretary might appreciate it if you turn in your paperwork on time. If you are sensitive to what the staff needs to make their jobs easier, they will be more willing to help make your job run smoother.

Paraprofessionals

Instructional aides can offer so much support to your classroom that you will soon wonder how you could survive without them. Yet aides can also cause you additional work. Be willing to offer constant support and guidance to your instructional aides.

Define their job descriptions. Decide whether they will tutor students, work with students who have been absent, check homework, assist in classroom design and layout, or help with record keeping. Get to know your aides and find out where they feel comfortable. If an aide hates math, do not ask that aide to tutor a small math group. Find out if the aide feels he or she could use more training, and then work with the site administrator to send the aide for additional training. This helps the aide feel valued as a professional, not just as an assistant.

Develop a schedule so that instructional aides know what they are responsible for doing when they are in your room. This will decrease the amount of time they spend asking you questions while you are working with students.

Volunteers

Parent and community volunteers can add much to your classroom. In the beginning of the school year, figure out what kind of help you need to make your classroom more efficient and balanced. You may need help filing papers, making copies, cutting out objects, laminating, making phone calls, or listening to students reading aloud. Perhaps some volunteers can visit the classroom to share their talents or careers. Once you identify your needs, send letters home asking for help. You may be amazed at the response. Many parents and community members may choose to volunteer. If only one person or a few people choose to volunteer, don't take it personally. Many people are extremely busy and simply do not have time to volunteer.

Before working with volunteers, ask the school administrator whether there are any school policies regarding volunteers (such as required check-in at the office prior to working in the classroom) or whether there is a volunteer handbook. After you have discussed school policies, welcome volunteers into your classroom with open arms. Make a schedule that explains when volunteers should come to class and what they will be doing. Keep an open line of communication with all volunteers, and you will find that they will be a great source of support to you throughout the year.

Community at Large

The community at large is a quiet, yet large, group of people on the fringes of every school's campus. These people are not directly involved in the school, yet they are very interested in it. The community at large includes city council members, local law enforcement officials, senior citizens who live close to the school, and of course the local newspaper.

These individuals can be your greatest allies and supporters if they are included in your communication efforts. You don't need to make an aggressive effort to establish contact with them, but when your paths do cross, invite them into your classroom or ask if they would like to receive your monthly newsletter. When you hold special reading days, invite a city council person to read aloud to your students. When you plan a career day, ask a local policeman or a reporter to come and talk to your class. Become pen pals with a local senior citizen group. When you make these small gestures, community members will feel included in your educational program, and their positive attitude toward you as an educator will trickle out to others around them. These days, public education can use as much public relations help as possible.

Worthwhile Web Sites

The following Web sites provide forums for teacher communication, information, and resources:

American Teachers (www.americanteachers.com)
Middle School Net (www.middleschool.net)
School House Talk Net (www.schoolhousetalk.com)
TeacherWeb (www.teacherweb.com)
Teaching.com (www.teaching.com)

A LAST LOOK AT THE TEACHER ■ AS A COMMUNICATOR

Being a good communicator is the foundation of being a good teacher. This chapter has examined some of the ways you can increase your effectiveness as a teacher by communicating well with students, parents, administrators, and many others. No one can become a strong communicator overnight.

Instead, it is something that all teachers, experienced and inexperienced, work at each year. Don't expect too much of yourself your first few years. Take time to reflect on how well your communication style is working with others and what needs to be changed or improved. Keep communicating clearly and often. You will reap the benefits.

■ RECOMMENDED READINGS

Barth, R. (1990). *Improving schools from within.* San Francisco: Jossey-Bass.

Palmer, P. (1998). *The courage to teach: Exploring the inner landscape of a teacher's life.* San Francisco: Jossey-Bass.

Sergiovanni, T. (1999). *Building community in schools.* San Francisco: Jossey-Bass.

Questions for Reflection ———————

What kind of strategies can I use to communicate effectively with my students?

_____

_____

_____

_____

How might I organize the back-to-school night to effectively communicate my messages to parents?

_____

_____

_____

_____

How can parent conferences be used to improve communication efforts?

_____

_____

_____

_____

How can I use technology in this effort to communicate?

_____

_____

_____

_____

Teacher as a Learner

"HOW CAN I REFINE MY PRACTICE?"

■ **TEACHING IS LEARNING**

By now, you have probably figured out that everything you need to know about teaching was not contained in your teacher preparation program. In fact, you may be worried that your preparation is still not complete. Remember: You are not alone. No new teacher comes into the classroom knowing everything. Most veteran teachers would readily admit that even after several years of teaching, they don't feel they have learned everything there is to know about teaching. Several factors contribute to this phenomenon:

> Remember: You are not alone. No new teacher comes into the classroom knowing everything.

- Teaching is complex.
- Teaching is dynamic.
- Teaching can be isolating.

Teaching Is Complex

Everyone who enters the field of teaching needs time and support to develop the intricate balance of knowledge, skills, and strategies necessary to be effective. Many states acknowledge this complexity and have created specific teaching standards that describe what teachers should know and do. Danielson (1996) expanded these standards in her book *Enhancing Professional Practice: A Framework for Teaching*. These standards look beyond the *what* of teaching (subject matter) and specifically address the *how* of teaching, reflecting the best practices of effective educators. Teaching standards typically address the skills and dispositions that are necessary to effectively organize curriculum, provide instruction, assess student learning, manage a classroom, and meet the needs of all students. Using teaching standards as a framework for improvement, teachers can refine their professional skills with practice, feedback, and support.

Teaching Is Dynamic

Being a teacher means that you will be faced with change on an ongoing basis—changes in curriculum, changes in the "best" teaching strategies, changes in student characteristics, changes in curriculum requirements, and changes in the school in which you teach. Studies show that teachers who succeed in adapting to these inevitable changes are those who consider themselves to be continuous learners—teachers who are interested in their own continuous improvement. Just as physicians keep current in medical interventions and research for the sake of their patients, these teachers embrace and commit to ongoing learning and improvement for the sake of their students.

Teaching Can Be Isolating

Isolation can limit the amount of exposure a teacher has to other strategies, solutions, and supports that can improve teaching. It is not unusual for teachers to arrive at school, enter their classrooms, close their doors, and proceed to teach the entire day without any significant interactions with their colleagues. As a beginning teacher, you must avoid this isolation from the start. Studies clearly demonstrate that effective teachers find ways to stay connected with their colleagues and other professionals. They don't work in isolation but rather work in partnership with others to understand the content of their teaching, find best practices for teaching that content, and reflect on their effectiveness.

Professional development can help you deal with the constant change and risk of isolation. *Professional development* is a general term that describes all activities in various content areas that lead to improved practice in teaching. As a beginning teacher, take advantage of these activities so that you can continue to grow as a teacher, be supported in that growth, and stay connected to others in the process. This chapter outlines a variety of ways you can accomplish these goals. It highlights the common forms of support, ways to increase your instructional skills, and strategies for staying connected to others through collaborative learning activities that affect student achievement.

> **Studies clearly demonstrate that effective teachers find ways to stay connected with their colleagues and other professionals.**

FINDING AND USING ■ SUPPORT AS A NEW TEACHER

As a beginning teacher, you must identify existing resources for support. Be sure to check with your district or school to see what support is available to you as a new teacher. Most states now require districts to provide some type of induction program to support beginning teachers.

Teacher Induction Programs

Induction programs offer a number of experiences and supports to help teachers successfully develop the qualities of effective teaching. These programs typically focus on classroom management, organization and delivery of instruction, and effective teaching strategies. Many induction programs are guided by national or state teaching standards.

The goal of an induction program is not to evaluate you as a new teacher; it is to support you in your journey to becoming a competent teacher. To provide this support, many induction programs pair beginning teachers with mentors (more experienced teachers). The role of these mentors (sometimes called *support providers*) is to guide beginning teachers through their first year or two of teaching and support them as they learn the skills and strategies of effective teaching.

> **The goal of an induction program is not to evaluate you as a new teacher; it is to support you in your journey to becoming a competent teacher.**

Figure 9.1, which illustrates the reflective learning cycle, shows the typical format of the activities you might experience within an induction program. You may begin the reflective learning cycle by designing a lesson plan that embeds a specific teaching strategy (*plan*). After you use the strategy with your students (*teach*), you would discuss the outcomes with your mentor (*reflect*). Finally, you would use the conclusions from the discussion to adjust the way you will use the strategy with your students in the future (*apply*). This plan-teach-reflect-apply process enables you to examine and improve your teaching practices with the help of your mentor. Some induction programs also use other learning activities, such as classroom observations and professional development workshops.

Figure 9.1   Reflective Learning Cycle

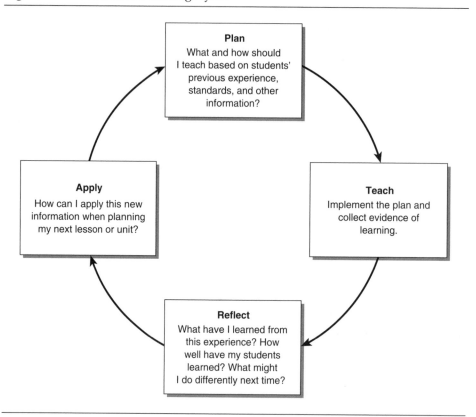

SOURCE: Adapted from *Mentoring Beginning Teachers: Guiding, Reflecting, Coaching,* by Jean Boreen, Mary K. Johnson, Donna Niday, and Joe Potts; Copyright © 2000, with permission of Stenhouse Publishers.

Alternative Support Programs

If your school or district does not have a formal induction program, pursue other sources of support for new teachers:

• *Ask your principal or other colleagues to pair you with a more experienced teacher.* Through your observations of this teacher, you may discover a professional who is particularly adept at managing the classroom, engaging the students, or using assessment information. You might ask this teacher for feedback on your ideas. Most teachers are happy to share information.

• *Use online mentor and support systems.* Teachers Network (teachers network.org/ntol/) and Classroom Connect (cu.classroom.com) are two examples.

- *Link with other new teachers in your district.*

- *Attend district workshops and inservices.* Use these opportunities to meet other teachers and get connected to others who teach similar grades and courses.

- *Check with a local university* to see if it offers programs to assist new teachers.

BUILDING YOUR TEACHING ABILITIES   ■

Even if you are participating in an induction program, you will also need to continually develop your professional skills. In fact, many states ensure this growth by requiring all teachers to participate in professional development hours prior to renewing their credentials. Many options are available for stimulating professional growth: workshops and inservices, advanced degree programs, embedded professional growth, and distance learning. These options differ in focus, structure, and setting.

Workshops and Inservices

The most common type of learning activity is traditionally provided through workshops and inservices. Districts frequently offer these workshops during professional development days that are scheduled one or two times each year. You may be asked to attend these workshops during school (by being released from class by a substitute) or after school.

First Week Flag

Get Organized for Your Professional Learning

As a teacher, you will be attending many professional development activities, including those required by your school or district. Sometimes the number of handouts provided during these learning sessions becomes overwhelming. Before the year begins and time gets away from you, get organized for your professional learning. Create a learning log or portfolio of your professional development experiences by organizing a three-ring binder or developing a set of files in a file cabinet. You may establish categories in advance (e.g., classroom management, literacy, and instructional strategies). If you get organized before you get busy, you'll be able to turn to a single resource instead of searching through a pile of files when you want to reflect on your learning experiences.

The information provided in workshops and inservices may range from broad topics that are indirectly connected to your teaching situation to very specific topics that are directly connected to your classroom needs. The key to productive workshops and inservices is what you do with the information after you leave the workshop. Ideally, you receive follow-up training, either in an additional workshop or through on-site support designed to help you use the strategy. However, if you attend only a single-session workshop, be sure to connect with a fellow teacher to discuss how you might apply the information in your classroom. You might ask the instructor for permission to contact him or her after the training for assistance in implementing the information.

Advanced Degree Programs

Many teachers choose to continue their formal education to obtain a master's or doctoral degree. Districts frequently acknowledge advanced degrees with additional pay on the salary schedule. In addition to the financial benefits, what you learn in a quality master's program can be highly valuable. A well-designed master's program provides a balance of research and application and usually engages participants in an in-depth study of a particular area, such as curriculum or leadership.

Before embarking on an advanced degree program, be sure that you are comfortable with your current workload. Decide whether you can devote several hours per week to your studies without sacrificing the quality of your teaching. You may choose to wait until you have taught for a few years before starting an advanced degree program. Fully devote yourself to your induction program and the process of developing as a beginning teacher before you complete the coursework you need to keep up your credentials.

Embedded Professional Growth

Workshops, inservices, and advanced degree programs have something in common: They all tend to focus on the needs of individual teachers but may not directly affect your practice in the classroom. In addition, they don't necessarily involve improvement-focused interactions with other teachers.

Another approach to staff development is embedded professional growth—working together with other teachers, focusing on the students' needs, and engaging in learning activities designed to positively affect students' achievement. This type of learning activity is not structured in the same format as traditional workshops. Instead, teams of teachers meet regularly during designated blocks of time to collaborate. These time blocks are embedded in the school schedule—before or after school or during common preparation periods.

When teacher teams meet, they identify common needs related to student learning, implement solutions to meet those needs, and determine the effectiveness of the solutions by analyzing the results.

Benefits of Embedded Professional Growth

➤ *Teachers feel they are part of a team that has a common mission.* They are all on the same page and working on the same agenda.

➤ *Teachers discover power in numbers.* When two or more teachers put their heads together to find a solution or create an end product, the final result is frequently of better quality than if each were working alone.

➤ *Teachers share a wealth of knowledge.* As a group, the teams stay abreast of strategies and information they need to do their jobs well and support each other as they change their classroom practices.

Teachers who participate in this embedded professional development not only improve their practice but also develop strong connections with others on the team. Best of all, as they collectively improve their teaching, they benefit the students and create systemwide improvements in their schools. The sidebar on page 190 titled "Benefits of Embedded Professional Growth" discusses more benefits.

Here are some examples of embedded professional development activities you can use to become connected with your colleagues and to enhance the achievement of your students:

- *Write curriculum.* Teachers can meet to map out a consistent curriculum that is aligned to the standards, determining the best approaches for integrating standards in their instruction. Teachers not only gain an opportunity to learn about the standards; they also experience synergy, teamwork, and a sense of accomplishment when working with colleagues.

- *Plan joint lessons and units.* Teachers can benefit from working collaboratively to create units and lessons that they in turn deliver to their students either separately or in teams. Working together to plan lessons and units introduces good ideas, divides the workload for each member of the team, and results in the development of higher-quality lessons and units for the students.

- *Develop common assessments.* As mentioned in Chapter 4, using ongoing assessments is necessary to determine whether your students are learning throughout your instruction. Teacher teams can work together to determine the expectations for teaching content standards and to design common assessments that can be used by the grade level or course team on a periodic basis. Teams can examine the effectiveness of the assessments and their teaching practices as well as observe improvements in student achievement.

- *Study lessons.* Teachers can bring particular lessons to the team and invite input from the team about the lesson design and teaching strategies included in the lesson. The team might ask how the lesson was designed, what standards the lesson intended to address, how the lesson assessed students' understanding, and what results occurred.

- *Review student work.* This approach is similar to studying lessons, but it places more emphasis on examining the results of instruction. After hearing a brief description of a lesson and assignment, the team examines students' work to help identify the impact of the instruction (Lewis, 1998).

- *Form study groups or book clubs.* Teams can meet to share research or discuss books about a common topic. Often, a facilitator oversees the team discussion and engages the team members in reflection.

- *Perform action research.* The team begins by identifying a particular need or problem in student achievement or classroom management. After the need or problem is defined, teams or individuals pose a research question, implement a solution based on their own research and ideas, and collect evidence of the solution's effectiveness. Action research may be completed by individuals or teams and may take place

Are All Online Courses of Equal Quality?

Online classes are offered through universities, professional organizations, and a number of commercial professional development vendors. However, all classes are not of equal quality. Use the following questions to evaluate distance learning courses:

➤ Is the course designed to give feedback to participants on a regular basis?

➤ Does the course guide the learner in the application of new concepts?

➤ What are the requirements of this course?

➤ Does the course offer opportunities for interaction?

➤ Will this course lead to changes in my practice as a teacher?

➤ Does the content of this class relate to my current teaching situation?

➤ Will my learning style mesh with this course?

➤ How will my learning be assessed?

➤ What are the technical requirements for participating in this class?

over weeks or months. Typically, conclusions from the action research are shared with others with the intent of improving classroom practice.

Distance Learning

Distance learning, which includes online professional development, teleconferencing, and independent study courses, is becoming increasingly available in the world of professional development. These options provide another alternative to afterschool or evening workshops and courses and allow you to participate in professional growth activities in a far more flexible format. Well-designed distance learning activities provide opportunities for interactions between the participants (teachers) and the instructor through electronic bulletin boards, real-time interactions (live chats), participant Web pages, e-mail, and discussion groups.

■ GETTING FEEDBACK ON YOUR TEACHING

Throughout your teaching experience, your instructional practice will be formally and informally observed and evaluated by principals and fellow teachers. Instead of feeling apprehensive about these experiences, think of them as opportunities to gain useful feedback on your teaching. Remember, all teachers must develop their skills throughout their careers. The key is to solicit feedback and act on it.

Worthwhile Web Sites

The following sites offer online professional development opportunities:

Association of Supervision and Curriculum Development (www.ascd.org)

Classroom Connect/Connected University (cu.classroom.com)

Educational Impact Online (www.eionline.net)

Harvard Graduate School Wide World (wideworld.pz.harvard.edu)

Pearson SkyLight Professional Development (www.lessonlab.com/index.cfm)

Tapped In (www.tappedin.org)

Classroom Observations

There are two types of classroom observations: informal and formal. As a classroom teacher, you will undoubtedly experience both types. If you understand the purpose and process for each type, you will be better prepared for them.

Informal Observations

Informal observations may occur at any time without prior scheduling. Your principal or administrators may conduct regular walk-through observations. Do not stop teaching during these casual visits. Administrators want to see classes in action, and they don't expect you to stop your instruction. Briefly acknowledging the administrator (e.g., saying "good morning") should suffice. If you are unsure of the best way to handle these visits, ask the administrator to clarify his or her expectations.

Formal Observations

During formal observations, administrators expect you to teach a complete lesson while they observe. Prior to the observation, you might need to provide a copy of your written lesson plan and seating chart to help your administrator connect students' names with their faces. Your administrator may look for the following during the observation:

- How your teaching objectives match the standards
- How you manage the classroom and instruction
- How you communicate with students (feedback, correction, etc.)
- What instructional strategies you use to enhance your students' learning
- What assessments (and checks for understanding) you use to monitor students' learning

Pre-Observation Conference. Many districts provide for a pre-observation conference between the teacher and the administrator-observer before a formal observation. During the conference, you share your lesson objectives and provide a context for the lesson. (For example, you might describe the activities you have conducted with students in previous lessons.) In addition, you might share a general profile of the class, including student achievement levels, special needs students, and any other pertinent information. This discussion provides good background information and helps the observer understand the rationale behind your teaching approach.

You might also ask the observer to observe a specific aspect of your teaching during the class. For example, if you know that you need to improve your feedback to students, ask the observer to evaluate your practices and provide you with input after the observation. Asking your administrator for constructive criticism demonstrates that you are interested in continuously improving your instructional skills.

Post-Observation Conference. Following your observation, it is customary for the administrator to review his or her observations with you. The observer might ask you some clarifying questions or share key points about the observation. Be sure to solicit specific feedback on any area of your teaching that you wish to enhance. For example, you may have used think-alouds to help students understand how they can approach a math problem. Explain why you used the think-alouds and ask the observer for specific feedback on how well the strategy worked.

Formal Evaluations

Your district probably considers beginning teachers to be probationary employees. You will be formally evaluated each year until you achieve tenure status.

During a formal evaluation, your administrator writes a report or completes a form that documents your performance relative to the expectations for all teachers in the district. This formal evaluation summarizes many observations that have taken place throughout the school year and indicates your level of performance in a number of areas. The report usually notes your strengths and your areas in need of improvement. In addition to rating your performance as a teacher, the administrator makes a recommendation regarding your employment. Typical recommendations include rehiring you as a probationary teacher, submitting your name for tenure status, or not recommending you for rehire.

The administrator shares the evaluation with you and places it in your personnel file. Most districts will offer you an opportunity to respond to the evaluation. Do your best to remain open to your administrator's suggestions. Ask clarifying questions if there are elements of the formal evaluation that seem unclear.

Use the Five R's When Selecting Professional Development

1. *Rigor.* Does it challenge you to examine your practice? Does it help you discover how you might improve as a professional?

2. *Research and Relevance.* Is it connected to your needs as a professional and the needs of your students? Is it connected to your schoolwide mission and goals? Does it offer an opportunity to examine your specific teaching situation?

3. *Reflective.* Does it foster reflective practice? Do you have the opportunity to interact with others and get feedback on your learning?

4. *Responsiveness.* Is it available and convenient? Does it engage you as a learner? Does the instructor take into account your learning needs and teaching context?

5. *Results.* Has the achievement of your students been affected by this learning experience?

■ GAINING THE MOST FROM PROFESSIONAL DEVELOPMENT

As you can see, you have numerous opportunities to grow professionally as a teacher. Following are some simple guidelines to help you decide which path is the best for you:

• *Find activities that are compatible with your learning style.* Teachers, like children, learn best when instruction is geared toward their specific learning style. For example, if you enjoy group discussions, don't sign up for an online class that offers discussion strands rather than live chats.

• *Choose activities that connect to what you need to know and do.* Don't fall into the habit of taking just any class or workshop for the sake of earning graduate units. If you don't feel that a workshop or class will directly benefit you and your students, look elsewhere. Sadly, many teachers warm seats in workshops, read their newspapers, and do not engage in activities.

- *Seek quality learning experiences.* Some courses and workshops offer higher quality than others. Be a good consumer; make sure you get a good return on your investment of time and money.

KEEPING CURRENT WITH BEST PRACTICES ■

As professionals, teachers have an obligation to keep current with best practices. By joining professional organizations and subscribing to professional journals, teachers can stay up to date in this ever changing profession.

Brain Bits

While the goal of professional development is to change your practice in the classroom, transferring the knowledge you gain in a workshop into your classroom is not automatic. Researchers examining brain-based teaching strategies (Hunter, 1982; Perkins & Salomon, 1988; West, Farmer, & Wolff, 1991) recommend the following techniques for enhancing the transfer of learning:

➤ *Attach new learning to prior learning.* Analyze the ways the new information is the same as or different from previously learned information.

➤ *Rehearse.* Practice new strategies within the workshop or training and solicit feedback from the instructor or your peers.

➤ *Brainstorm.* During or following a professional learning session, work with colleagues to list ways you can implement the newly learned strategies in your classroom.

➤ *Reflect.* Spend time reflecting about what you learned during the experience. Share your reflections (orally or in writing) with a group. Meet periodically to discuss your successes or challenges in implementing new strategies.

Professional Organizations

One of the best ways to keep current with trends and new strategies in teaching is to become a member of a professional organization. Most organizations have journal subscriptions, and many have Web sites, Listservs, and other valuable benefits of membership. See Worthwhile Web Sites (page 196) for some well-known educational professional organizations and their Web site addresses.

Professional Reading

Becoming a member of a professional organization will likely provide you with the opportunity to receive literature on current issues in education, best practices in teaching, and resources for instruction. In addition to this information, be sure to read a number of professional books. Numerous educational books are available at popular bookstores or through online booksellers.

┌───┐
Worthwhile Web Sites

Visit the sites of these well-known educational professional organizations:

American Federation of Teachers (www.aft.org/index.html)
Association for Supervision and Curriculum Development (www.ascd.org)
International Reading Association (www.reading.org)
National Board for Professional Teaching Standards (www.nbpts.org)
National Council of Teachers of English (www.ncte.org)
National Council of Teachers of Mathematics (www.nctm.org)
National Education Association (www.nea.org)
National Science Teachers Association (www.nsta.org)
Phi Delta Kappa International (www.pdkintl.org)
└───┘

■ LOOKING AHEAD

As you move along in your career, you may choose to pursue certification through the National Board for Professional Teaching Standards. This certification is often viewed as the "Good Housekeeping Seal of Approval" of teaching. The process for becoming board certified involves a rigorous, 10-month, reflective study of your own practice and the completion of specific activities designed to demonstrate that you meet the national standards. Teachers who have completed this process believe that it is one of the most in-depth and valuable professional growth experiences in which they have ever participated. For more information on National Board Certification, visit www.nbpts.org/.

■ A LAST LOOK AT THE TEACHER AS A LEARNER

There are many teachers in the world, and each and every one has a different set of strengths and weaknesses. The key is to figure out your own strengths and weaknesses through your own reflection and feedback from others. Identify your specific needs and seek ways to improve them. Don't worry about admitting that you don't know it all—remember that nobody does, especially in the first few years of teaching. Take advantage of learning opportunities throughout your career, including those that come from connecting with the experienced teachers in your school and district. Being a professional educator is about growing, sharing, and continuous learning. It's about knowing that whatever you do to improve your teaching is for one reason—your students.

■ RECOMMENDED READINGS

Danielson, C. (1996). *Enhancing professional practice: A framework for teaching.* Alexandria, VA: Association for Supervision and Curriculum Development.
Williamson, B. (1998). *A first-year teacher's guidebook: An educational recipe book for success.* Sacramento, CA: Dynamic Teaching Company.

Questions for Reflection

What structures and supports do I need to grow as a professional educator?

_____

_____

_____

_____

_____

In what area would I like to focus my professional growth at this time?

_____

_____

_____

_____

_____

What are some ways I can get connected with others in my school?

_____

_____

_____

_____

_____

Conclusion: Finding Your Own Style and Voice

There are as many different kinds of teachers as there are students. They come in all shapes and sizes, and no two teachers are alike. When you begin teaching, it is helpful to find mentors and to watch how veteran teachers master this profession. Yet as the months go by in your first year, and the first year turns to the second and then the third, the time will come for you to step out from the shadows of the "new teacher" label and feel comfortable with who and what you are as a teacher. You come to the classroom with a unique set of talents and gifts, and it doesn't do any good to compare yourself to the teacher next door or the one that just got recognized at an award banquet.

Instead, allowing your own teaching style to emerge and flourish will be energizing to you both professionally and personally. At a certain point in a teaching profession, all teachers begin to rely on their instincts and their gut reactions more than their teacher's manuals. It is at this point that your style and voice will surface and you will find yourself speaking up more in meetings and feeling more confident and empowered in your classroom and school community.

Teaching is an exciting and wild ride. Do it well. Give it all you've got. Buckle your seat belt. Know you are touching the future each and every day. Have fun!

Bibliography

Adams, M. J. (1990). *Beginning to read: Thinking and learning about print.* Cambridge, MA: MIT.

Allington, R. (2001). *What really matters for struggling readers.* New York: Longman.

Anderson, L. W., Krathwohl, D. R., Airasian, P. W., Cruikshank, K. A., Mayer, R. E., Pintrich, P. R., et al. (2000). *Taxonomy for learning, teaching, and assessing: A revision of Bloom's taxonomy of educational objectives.* Boston: Allyn & Bacon.

Anderson, R. C., Wilson, P. T., & Fielding, L. G. (1988, Summer). Growth in reading and how children spend their time outside of school. *Reading Research Quarterly, 23*(3), 285–303.

Andrade, G. H. (2000). Using rubrics to promote thinking and learning. *Educational Leadership, 57*(5), 13–18.

Armstrong, T. (1994). *Multiple intelligences in the classroom.* Alexandria, VA: Association for Supervision and Curriculum Development.

Armstrong, T. (1998). *Awakening genius in the classroom.* Alexandria, VA: Association for Supervision and Curriculum Development.

Atwood, V. A., & Wilen, W. W. (1991). Wait time and effective social studies instruction: What can research in science education tell us? *Social Education, 55*(3), 179–181. (ERIC Document Reproduction Service No. EJ430537)

Barth, R. (1990). *Improving schools from within.* San Francisco: Jossey-Bass.

Barth, R. (2003). *Lessons learned: Shaping relationships and the culture of the workplace.* Thousand Oaks, CA: Corwin Press.

Beattie, M. (1998). *Finding your way home: A soul survival kit.* San Francisco: Harper SanFrancisco.

Berman, T. (2003). *Purchasing and selecting school lighting.* Dayton, OH: School Planning and Management.

Bernstein, A. (2001). *Emotional vampires.* New York: McGraw-Hill.

Billmeyer, R. (1996). *Teaching reading in the content areas: If not me, then who?* Aurora, CO: Mid-continent Regional Educational Laboratory.

Bloom, B. S. (Ed.). (1956). *Taxonomy of educational objectives: The classification of educational goals: Handbook I, cognitive domain.* New York: Longman.

Blythe, T., & researchers and teachers of the Teaching for Understanding Project. (1998). *The teaching for understanding guide.* San Francisco: Jossey-Bass.

Boreen, J., Johnson, M. K., Niday, D., & Potts, J. (2000). *Mentoring beginning teachers.* York, ME: Stenhouse.

Boyer, E. L. (1983). *High school: A report on secondary education in America.* New York: Harper & Row.

Brandt, R. (1998a). Listen first: Engaging parents in the community in schools. *Educational Leadership, 55*(8), 25–30.

Brandt, R. (1998b). *Powerful learning.* Alexandria, VA: Association for Supervision and Curriculum Development.

Breathnach, S. B. (1995). *Simple abundance: A daybook of comfort and joy.* New York: Warner.

Burke, K. (2005). *How to assess authentic learning* (4th ed.). Thousand Oaks, CA: Corwin Press.

Caine, R., & Caine, G. (1991). *Making connections: Teaching and the human brain.* Alexandria, VA: Association for Supervision and Curriculum Development.

Campbell, B. (1994). *The multiple intelligences handbook: Lesson plans and more.* Stanwood, WA: Campbell.

Campbell, B., & Campbell, L. (1999). *Multiple intelligences and student achievement: Success stories from six schools.* Alexandria, VA: Association for Supervision and Curriculum Development.

Canter & Associates. (1998). *First class teacher: Successful strategies for new teachers.* Santa Monica, CA: Author.

Carr, J., & Harris, D. (2001). *Succeeding with standards.* Alexandria, VA: Association for Supervision and Curriculum Development.

Carter, C. (1997). Why reciprocal teaching. *Educational Leadership, 53,* 64–68.

Cooper, J. D., Boschken, I., McWilliams, J., & Pistochini, L. (1997). Summary of research report, Soar to success: Teacher's manual, R2–R9.

Covey, S. (1990). *The 7 habits of highly effective people.* New York: Simon & Schuster.

Csikszentmihalyi, M. (1990). *Flow: The psychology of optimal experience.* New York: Harper & Row.

Cummings, C. (2000). *Winning strategies for classroom management.* Alexandria, VA: Association for Supervision and Curriculum Development.

Cunningham, A. E., & Stanovich, K. E. (1997). Early reading acquisition and its relation to reading experience and ability ten years later. *Developmental Psychology, 33*(6), 934–945.

Daggett, W. (1990, November). *Quality in education: A new collaborative initiative and process for change.* Seminar presented in Linden, MI.

Danielson, C. (1996). *Enhancing professional practice: A framework for teaching.* Alexandria, VA: Association for Supervision and Curriculum Development.

Darling-Hammond, L. (1997). *The right to learn: A blueprint for creating schools that work.* San Francisco: Jossey-Bass.

Darling-Hammond, L. (1998). Teacher learning that supports student learning. *Educational Leadership, 55*(5), 6–11.

De Amicis, B. (1999). *3 cheers for teaching: A guide to growing professionally and renewing your spirit.* Tucson, AZ: Zephyr.

Diamond, M. (1988). *Enriching heredity: The impact of the environment on the anatomy of the brain.* New York: Free Press.

Fogarty, R. (1995). *Integrating the curricula: A collection.* Thousand Oaks, CA: Corwin Press. (2nd ed. in production for 2008.)

Fogarty, R. (1997). *Problem-based learning and other curriculum models for the multiple intelligences classroom.* Thousand Oaks, CA: Corwin Press.

Fry, E. (1993). *Reading teacher's book of lists* (3rd ed.). Upper Saddle River, NJ: Prentice Hall.

Gage, F. (1997, April 24). *An enriched environment stimulates an increase in the number of nerve cells in brains of older mice.* Salk Institute, news release.

Gardner, H. (1983). *Frames of mind: The theory of multiple intelligences.* New York: Basic.

Gardner, H. (1991). *The unschooled mind: How children think and how schools should teach.* New York: Basic.

Gardner, H. (1993a). *Creating minds.* New York: Basic.

Gardner, H. (1993b). *Multiple intelligences: The theory in practice.* New York: Basic.

Goleman, D. (1995). *Emotional intelligence.* New York: Bantam.

Guskey, T. R. (2001). Fixing grading policies that undermine standards. *Education Digest, 66*(7), 16–21.

Guskey, T. R., & Bailey, J. M. (2001). *Developing grading and reporting systems for student learning: Experts in assessment.* Thousand Oaks, CA: Corwin Press.

Harris, D., & Carr, J. (1996). *How to use standards in the classroom.* Alexandria, VA: Association for Supervision and Curriculum Development.

Harris, J. (1998). *Virtual architecture: Designing and directing curriculum-based tele-computing.* Eugene, OR: International Society for Technology in Education.

Hart, L. (1983). *Human brain, human learning.* Kent, WA: Books for Educators.

Harvey, S., & Goudvis, A. (2000). *Strategies that work: Teaching comprehension to enhance understanding.* Portland, ME: Stenhouse.

Healy, J. M. (1990). *Endangered minds: Why our children don't think.* New York: Simon & Schuster.

Heide, A., & Stilborne, L. (1998). *The teacher's complete and easy guide to the Internet* (2nd ed.). New York: Teachers College Press.

Honig, B. (1996). *Teaching our children to read: The role of skills in a comprehensive reading program.* Thousand Oaks, CA: Corwin Press.

Hunter, M. C. (1982). *Mastery teaching.* El Segundo, CA: T.I.P.

Jacobs, H. H. (1989). *Interdisciplinary curriculum: Design and implementation.* Alexandria, VA: Association for Supervision and Curriculum Development.

Jacobs, H. H. (1999). *Breaking new ground in high school integrated curriculum.* Reston, VA: National Association of Secondary School Principals.

James, J. (1996). *Thinking in the future tense: Leadership skills for a new age.* New York: Simon & Schuster.

Johnson, D. W., & Johnson, R. T. (1999). *Learning together and alone: Cooperative, competitive, and individualistic learning.* Boston: Allyn & Bacon.

Johnson, D. W., Johnson, R. T., & Holubec, E. J. (1994). *Cooperative learning in the classroom.* Alexandria, VA: Association for Supervision and Curriculum Development.

Jones, F. (2000). *Tools for teaching.* Santa Cruz, CA: Fredric H. Jones & Associates.

Jonson, K. F. (2002). *The new elementary teacher's handbook.* Thousand Oaks, CA: Corwin Press.

Kazdin, A. E. (1973). The effect of vicarious reinforcement on attentive behavior in the classroom. *Journal of Applied Behavior Analysis, 6,* 71–78.

Keene, E., & Zimmermann, S. (1997). *Mosaic of thought: Teaching comprehension in a reader's workshop.* Portsmouth, NH: Heinemann.

Kendall, J. S., & Marzano, R. J. (1997). *Content knowledge: A compendium of standards and benchmarks for K–12 education* (2nd ed.). Alexandria, VA: Association for Supervision and Curriculum Development.

Kovalik, S. (1993). *ITI, the model: Integrated thematic instruction.* Kent, WA: Books for Educators.

Kralovec, E. (2001). *The end of homework: How homework disrupts families, overburdens children, and limits learning.* Boston: Beacon.

Krashen, S. (1993). *The power of reading.* Englewood, CO: Libraries Unlimited.

Lazear, D. (1994). *Multiple intelligence approaches to assessment.* Tucson, AZ: Zephyr.

LeDoux, J. E. (1996). *The emotional brain: The mysterious underpinnings of emotional life.* New York: Simon & Schuster.

Levine, M. (1994). *Educational care.* Cambridge, MA: Educational Publishers Service.

Lewin, L., & Shoemaker, B. (1998). *Great performances: Creating classroom-based assessment tasks.* Alexandria, VA: Association for Supervision and Curriculum Development.

Lewis, A. C. (1998). Student work. *Journal of Staff Development, 19*(4), 24–27.

Maas, J. (1999). *Power sleep: The revolutionary program that prepares your mind for peak performance.* New York: HarperCollins.

Madsen, C. H., Jr., Becker, W. C., & Thomas, D. R. (1968). Rules, praise, and ignoring: Elements of elementary classroom control. *Journal of Applied Behavior Analysis, 1,* 139–150.

Marzano, R. J., & Kendall, J. S. (1996). *A comprehensive guide to designing standards-based districts, schools, and classrooms.* Alexandria, VA: Association for Supervision and Curriculum Development.

Marzano, R. J., Pickering, D., & Pollock, J. (2001). *Classroom instruction that works: Research-based strategies for increasing student achievement.* Alexandria, VA: Association for Supervision and Curriculum Development.

Marzano, R. J., Whisler, J. S., Dean, C. B., & Pollock, J. E. (2000). *Effective instructional practices.* Aurora, CO: Mid-continent Regional Educational Laboratory.

Mitchell, R., Crawford, M., & Chicago Teachers Union Quest Center. (1995). *Learning in overdrive: Designing curriculum, instruction, and assessment from standards.* Golden, CO: Fulcrum Resources.

Moore, T. (1992). *Care of the soul.* New York: HarperPerennial.

Nelson, J., Lott, L., & Glenn, S. (2000). *Positive discipline in the classroom.* Roseville, CA: Prima.

Ogle, D. (1986). K-W-L: A teaching model that develops active reading of expository text. *The Reading Teacher, 39*(6), 564–571.

Palincsar, A. S., & Brown, A. L. (1984). Reciprocal teaching of comprehension: Fostering and comprehension monitoring activities. *Cognition and Instruction, 1*(2), 117–175.

Palmer, B. M., Codling, R. M., & Gambrell, L. B. (1994). In their own words: What elementary students have to say about motivation to read. *The Reading Teacher, 48*, 176–178.

Palmer, P. (1998). *The courage to teach: Exploring the inner landscape of a teacher's life.* San Francisco: Jossey-Bass.

Perkins, D. (1999). The many faces of constructivism. *Educational Leadership, 57*(3), 6–11.

Perkins, D. N., & Salomon, G. (1988). Teaching for transfer. *Educational Leadership, 46*(1), 22–32.

Pressley, M. (2002). *Reading instruction that works: The case for balanced teaching* (2nd ed.). New York: Guilford.

Pressley, M., & Afflerbach, P. (1995). *Verbal protocols of reading: The nature of constructively responsive reading.* Hillsdale, NJ: Erlbaum.

Richardson, C. (1999). *Take time for your life.* New York: Broadway Books.

Rominger, L., Heisinger, K., & Elkin, N. (2001). *Your first year as an elementary school teacher: Making the transition from total novice to a successful professional.* Roseville, CA: Prima.

Rominger, L., Laughrea, S., & Elkin, N. (2001). *Your first year as a high school teacher: Making the transition from total novice to a successful professional.* Roseville, CA: Prima.

Routman, R. (2003). *Reading essentials: The specifics you need to teach reading well.* Portsmouth, NH: Heinemann.

Rowe, M. B. (1972, April). Wait-time and rewards as instructional variables: Their influence in language, logic, and fate control. Paper presented at the National Association for Research in Science Teaching, Chicago, IL. (ERIC Document Reproduction Service No. ED061103)

Rowe, M. B. (1987). Wait time: Slowing down may be a way of speeding up. *American Educator, 11*(1), 38–43, 47. (ERIC Document Reproduction Service No. EJ351827)

Salvia, J., & Hughes, C. (1990). *Curriculum-based assessment.* New York: Macmillan.

Sapolsky, R. (1994). *Why zebras don't get ulcers.* New York: W. H. Freeman.

Schlechty, P. C. (1997). *Inventing better schools: An action plan for educational reform.* San Francisco: Jossey-Bass.

Schmoker, M. (1996). *RESULTS: The key to continuous school improvement.* Alexandria, VA: Association for Supervision and Curriculum Development.

Schmoker, M., & Marzano, R. J. (1999). Realizing the promise of standards-based education. *Educational Leadership, 56*(6), 17–21.

Schneider, M. (2002). *Do school facilities affect academic outcomes?* National Clearinghouse for Educational Facilities.

Schnick, T., & Knickelbine, M. (2000). *The Lexile framework: An introduction for educators.* Durham, NC: Metametrics.

Secretary's Commission on Achieving Necessary Skills (SCANS). (1991). *What work requires of schools: A SCANS report for America 2000.* Washington, DC: U.S. Department of Labor, Secretary's Commission on Achieving Necessary Skills.

Sergiovanni, T. (1999). *Building community in schools.* San Francisco: Jossey-Bass.

Silver, H., Strong, R., & Perini, M. (2001). *Tools for promoting active, in-depth learning* (2nd ed.). Ho-Ho-Kus, NJ: Thoughtful Education.

Slavin, R. E. (1995). *Cooperative learning* (2nd ed.). Boston: Allyn & Bacon.

Sousa, D. (2006). *How the brain learns* (3rd ed). Thousand Oaks, CA: Corwin Press.

Sprenger, M. (1999). *Learning and memory: The brain in action.* Alexandria, VA: Association for Supervision and Curriculum Development.

Stanovich, K. E. (1986). Matthew effects in reading: Some consequences of individual differences in the acquisition of literacy. *Reading Research Quarterly, 21,* 360–407.

Stiggins, R. (2001). *Student-involved classroom assessment* (3rd ed.). Upper Saddle River, NJ: Merrill Prentice Hall.

Strong, R. W., Silver, H. F., & Perini, M. J. (2001). *Teaching what matters most.* Alexandria, VA: Association for Supervision and Curriculum Development.

Sylwester, R. (1995). *A celebration of neurons: An educator's guide to the brain.* Alexandria, VA: Association for Supervision and Curriculum Development.

Tomlinson, C. A. (1995). *How to differentiate instruction in mixed-ability classrooms.* Alexandria, VA: Association for Supervision and Curriculum Development.

Trelease, J. (2001). *The read-aloud handbook.* New York: Penguin.

Wagner, A. D., Schacter, D. L., Rotte, M., Koutstaal, W., Maril, A., Dale, A. M., et al. (1998). Building memories: Remembering and forgetting of verbal experiences as predicted by brain activity. *Science, 281,* 1188–1191.

Weil, A. (1997). *8 weeks to optimum health.* New York: Alfred A. Knopf.

West, C. K., Farmer, J., & Wolff, P. M. (1991). *Instructional design: Implications from cognitive science.* Englewood Cliffs, NJ: Prentice Hall.

Wiggins, G., & McTighe, J. (1998). *Understanding by design.* Alexandria, VA: Association for Supervision and Curriculum Development.

Williamson, B. (1998). *A first-year teacher's guidebook: An educational recipe book for success.* Sacramento, CA: Dynamic Teaching Company.

Wolfe, P. (2001). *Brain matters: Translating research into classroom practice.* Alexandria, VA: Association for Supervision and Curriculum Development.

Wong, H., & Wong, R. (1998). *The first days of school.* Mountain View, CA: Harry Wong Publications.

Wooden, J. (2004). *My personal best: Life lessons from an all-American journey.* New York: McGraw-Hill.

Worthy, J. (2002). What makes intermediate-grade students want to read? *Reading Teacher, 55,* 568–569.

Index